Contents

Section 1: Initiating Your Ansible Journey

1. Welcome & What You'll Learn
2. Unveiling the Power of Ansible

Section 2: Setting the Foundation: Configuration and Core Concepts

3. Navigating Ansible's Configuration Realm, Part 1
4. Mastering the Anatomy of Ansible Configuration, Part 2
5. Demystifying YAML: A Comprehensive Dive, Part 1
6. Unraveling the Mysteries of YAML: Deep Dive, Part 2
7. Hands-On Exercise: Crafting YAML Wonders

Section 3: Mapping Your Territory: Ansible Inventory

8. Crafting Your Ansible Arsenal: Understanding Inventory
9. Practical Exercise: Crafting Your Inventory Arsenal
10. Inventory Alchemy: Exploring Formats and Structures
11. Forging Alliances: Grouping and Hierarchies in Inventory Management

Section 4: Harnessing the Power of Ansible Variables

12. Unleashing the Magic of Ansible Variables
13. Deciphering Variable Varieties
14. Capturing Triumphs: Variable Registration and Precedence, Unveiled, Part 1
15. Capturing Triumphs: Variable Registration and Precedence, Unveiled, Part 2
16. Scoping Out Variable Terrain
17. Peering into the Mystical Realm: Ansible's Magic Variables
18. The Saga of Ansible Facts Unfolded
19. Practical Application: Variable Mastery and Fact Finding Expedition

Section 5: Orchestrating with Ansible Playbooks

20. Crafting the Symphony: Introduction to Ansible Playbooks
21. Fine-Tuning Your Harmony: Playbook Verification Techniques
22. Tuning In to Quality: Ansible-lint for Playbook Perfection
23. Hands-On Exercise: Mastering Playbook Composition

24. Navigating Choices: Conditional Logic in Ansible
25. Crafting Dynamic Scenarios: Advanced Conditionals and Variable Utilization
26. Practical Exercise: Crafting Conditional Masterpieces
27. Embracing Repetition: Looping Constructs, Part 1
28. Diving Deeper into Iterations: Looping Constructs, Part 2
29. Hands-On Challenge: Iterative Brilliance with Ansible Loops

Section 6: Harnessing the Power of Ansible Modules

30. Unveiling the Arsenal: Exploring Ansible Modules, Part 1
31. Expanding Your Toolkit: Exploring Ansible Modules, Part 2
32. Illuminating Possibilities: Introduction to Ansible Plugins
33. Coding Expedition: Exploring Ansible Modules in Action

Section 7: Orchestrating with Finesse: Handlers, Roles, and Collections

34. Mastering the Art of Responsiveness: An Insight into Handlers
35. Crafting Reusable Solutions: Understanding Ansible Roles, Part 1
36. Scaling Your Infrastructure: Understanding Ansible Roles, Part 2
37. Embracing Innovation: Unveiling Ansible Collections
38. Practical Challenge: Harnessing the Power of Handlers, Roles, and Collections

Section 8: Journey into the Advanced Realm

39. Unveiling the Secrets of Templating
40. Crafting Dynamic Configurations with Jinja2 Templates: Hands-On Demo, Part 1
41. Crafting Dynamic Configurations with Jinja2 Templates: Hands-On Demo, Part 2

~ *Conclusion*

Section 1: Initiating Your Ansible Journey

Welcome & What You'll Learn

Embarking on Your Ansible Expedition

Greetings, and welcome to the exhilarating world of Ansible! If you're ready to revolutionize the way you manage IT infrastructure, you've come to the right place. Whether you're a seasoned systems administrator, a developer venturing into DevOps, or an IT enthusiast curious about automation, this book, "Getting Started with Ansible: A Hands-On Guide to DevOps for Absolute Beginners", will be your trusty compass on this transformative journey.

Why Ansible? The Call of Automation

Picture yourself faced with dozens, even hundreds, of servers to configure, packages to install, applications to roll out. The old ways of manual configuration, scripting your way around problems, and those sleepless nights spent battling production fires – these are the dragons Ansible is designed to slay.

With Ansible, you'll:

- **Simplify Complexity:** Manage large-scale infrastructure with elegant, easy-to-read instructions.

- **Boost Efficiency:** Save time and prevent those frustrating, error-prone manual tasks.
- **Ensure Consistency:** Relax, knowing that your systems will be in the desired state every time.
- **Collaborate effortlessly:** Ansible's human-readable format builds bridges between development and operations teams.

Unleashing Your Automation Superpowers

As you venture through this book, you'll gain the following superpowers:

- **Ansible Foundations:** The inner workings of Ansible, covering installation, its key concepts, and the gentle art of configuring it for success.
- **YAML Mastery:** Discover the structured data language that breathes life into your Ansible instructions.
- **Inventory Management:** Learn how to organize your servers and other devices for easy targeting by Ansible.
- **Mastering Variables:** Make your Ansible instructions even more flexible and dynamic by cleverly injecting variables for specific scenarios.
- **Playbook Supremacy:** Craft powerful Ansible Playbooks – like recipes for automation – filled with tasks, logic, and iterations.
- **Harnessing Modules:** Unleash the vast library of pre-built Ansible modules to perform common tasks across a multitude of systems.
- **Advanced Techniques:** Level up with templating, Ansible roles, and collections to create truly modular and adaptable solutions.

It's All About the Hands-On Experience

This book isn't just about reading; it's about doing. Theoretical concepts are great, but true mastery comes from rolling up your sleeves. Each chapter comes equipped with practical exercises and code challenges to turn knowledge into real-world skill. By the end of this book, you'll have built a firm foundation and the practical prowess to start automating your infrastructure with confidence.

Additional Resources

To give you the most well-rounded Ansible experience, here's a treasure chest of resources:

- **The Official Ansible Documentation:** https://docs.ansible.com/
- **Ansible Examples Repository:** https://github.com/ansible/ansible-examples
- **Ansible Galaxy:** https://galaxy.ansible.com/ (Community hub for roles and modules)

Are You Ready?

The path ahead will be exciting, empowering, and filled with the sweet satisfaction of tasks done right – automatically. Get those fingers warmed up. Let's start exploring the awesome power of Ansible!

Unveiling the Power of Ansible

In the previous chapter, we caught a glimpse of the automation revolution Ansible empowers you to lead. Now, it's time to delve deeper into why Ansible has become the darling of the DevOps world. Let's unbox those special qualities that make it such a compelling tool.

The Ansible Advantage: What Makes It Shine

1. **Simplicity at its Core:** Ansible isn't here to make things complicated. It believes in a 'batteries-included' approach, meaning you can start automating right away without having to install tons of extra software. Its instructions are written in plain-English-like language, making it incredibly beginner-friendly.
2. **Agentless Magic:** Unlike some other configuration tools, Ansible doesn't need special software (agents) to be pre-installed on the machines you want to manage. It primarily uses SSH (for Linux/Unix) and WinRM (for Windows) to communicate – protocols that are likely already open in your environment. This makes Ansible lightweight and easier to introduce into your infrastructure.
3. **Powerfully Push-Based:** Ansible works by 'pushing out' your desired configurations to target machines. This means your central Ansible control machine orchestrates the changes. It brings a heightened level of control and predictability to your operations.
4. **Idempotence: The Quest for Consistency:** A fancy word, but here's what it means: If you run an Ansible instruction multiple times, it intelligently figures out if the desired state is already achieved. If so, it won't make unnecessary changes, ensuring your systems stay exactly as intended while preventing disruptive updates.

Real-World Ansible in Action

Let's move away from the abstract and imagine some of the ways you might unleash Ansible:

- **Software Installation and Updates:** "Install the latest web server package on all production servers, but only after business hours" - Ansible does this with ease.
- **Configuration Enforcement:** "Make sure our firewall has these 5 security rules enabled across our entire fleet of machines." Ansible ensures compliance.
- **Cloud Orchestration:** "Spin up 10 new virtual machines with our standard application stack." Ansible can make your infrastructure elastic and responsive to demand.
- **CI/CD Integration:** Ansible works harmoniously with tools like Jenkins to automate testing, building, and deployment of your software projects.

The DevOps Difference

Ansible speaks the language of DevOps. Let's see how it fits into this philosophy:

- **Infrastructure as Code:** Ansible's instructions (Playbooks, etc.) are text files. This means you can version control them like software code, enabling collaboration, rollbacks if needed, and a transparent history of changes.
- **Bridging Gaps:** Ansible brings together developers (who want to deploy new code fast) and operations teams (who need stability). Ansible provides the common language to define and automate infrastructure needs.
- **Speed and Reliability:** Automation done right with Ansible means faster deployments, fewer errors, and more time to innovate rather than fighting fires.

Additional Resources

- **Ansible Case Studies:** Get inspired by real-world examples of Ansible in action: https://www.ansible.com/case-studies
- **DevOps - Wikipedia:** Get a solid foundation on the DevOps philosophy: https://en.wikipedia.org/wiki/DevOps

Embracing the Automation Shift

Ansible isn't just a tool; it's a mindset change. It's about embracing infrastructure that's defined, managed, and versioned like the software it supports. Are you ready to step into this new paradigm? Turn the page, and let's start setting up Ansible and exploring its core concepts!

Section 2:

Setting the Foundation: Configuration and Core Concepts

Navigating Ansible's Configuration Realm, Part 1

Welcome, explorer! In this chapter, we embark on a journey into the realm of Ansible configuration. Think of this as understanding the compass and map that will guide your automation expeditions. We'll cover installing Ansible, deciphering the main configuration file, and setting up communication with the systems you want to manage.

Your Control Machine: Setting Up Base Camp

Before you can start commanding your infrastructure, you'll need a base of operations – your Ansible control machine. This is the computer where you'll install Ansible and from where you'll issue instructions. Here's a quick overview:

- **Operating System:** Ansible plays well with Linux (e.g., Ubuntu, CentOS), macOS, or Windows (with Windows Subsystem for Linux).
- **Installation:** Usually, you can install using your system's package manager like `apt-get` or `yum`. Refer to the official Ansible installation guide for tailored instructions.

Note: Throughout the book, we might assume a Linux-based control machine, but the concepts translate easily to other supported environments.

Demystifying the Heart of the Operation: ansible.cfg

The `ansible.cfg` file is your Ansible control center. It typically lives in `/etc/ansible/ansible.cfg` or in the same directory as your playbooks. Let's peek inside and understand some of the crucial sections:

- **[defaults]** This section sets up general defaults for Ansible's behavior:
    - **inventory:** The path to your Ansible inventory file (we'll dive into inventory in the next chapter).
    - **remote_user:** The default username Ansible uses to connect to your managed machines.
    - **ask_pass:** Whether Ansible should prompt you for an SSH password.
- **[privilege_escalation]** Settings for if you need superuser powers (think 'sudo' on Linux) for certain tasks.

Tip: Initially, don't worry about modifying everything in `ansible.cfg`. We'll point out relevant settings as we progress!

Mapping the Terrain: Host and Group Management

Ansible lets you precisely target the machines (hosts) you want to control and group them logically. Think of hosts as individual servers and groups as collections of servers that share a common role (like "webservers" or "databases"). You'll usually define these in your Ansible Inventory file, but for quick tests, Ansible lets you specify hosts directly on the command line.

The `-i` Option: Your Temporary Map

For fast experiments, you can use the `-i` option with Ansible commands to give it a comma-separated list of hosts. Example:

```
ansible -i "192.168.1.10,192.168.1.20" -m ping all
```

This tells Ansible to run the "ping" module (a simple connectivity check) on two specified IP addresses.

Additional Resources

- **Ansible Installation Guide:** [https://docs.ansible.com/ansible/latest/installation_guide/intro_installation.html]
- **Understanding the Ansible Configuration File:** https://docs.ansible.com/ansible/latest/reference_appendices/config.html

Get Ready To Explore!

In the next chapter, we'll continue exploring `ansible.cfg` and build out your Ansible inventory – the structured map of your managed systems.

Mastering the Anatomy of Ansible Configuration, Part 2

In the previous chapter, we began our exploration of Ansible's configuration file (`ansible.cfg`) and how to manage connections to our targets. Now, let's delve deeper into specific sections of the configuration file that will greatly enhance how you wield Ansible for automation.

Remote Management Mastery

- **Connection Settings:** Ansible primarily uses SSH for the control machine to connect to your managed nodes. Fine-tune connection behavior:
    - **host_key_checking:** How Ansible handles verifying new host keys (Security aspect).
    - **timeout:** How long Ansible waits for connections to establish before giving up.
- **SSH Pipelining:** (For efficiency) Enable `pipelining` to speed up communication and reduce connection overhead, especially in high-latency environments.

Becoming a Privilege Escalation Pro

Many tasks require superuser powers on your managed hosts. Ansible gives you granular control over how to achieve this:

- **[privilege_escalation] (continued):**
    - **become:** Whether to escalate privileges at all.
    - **become_method:** Pick your weapon: `sudo`, `su`, `doas`, etc.
    - **become_user:** Specifies which user to become (usually 'root').

- o **become_ask_pass:** If Ansible should prompt you for the escalation password.

Crafting Custom Strategies

Some environments have unique requirements, and Ansible lets you adapt. Introduce the concept of strategies:

- **[strategy]** For fine-grained control of how tasks are executed on hosts:
  - o **free:** The default – tasks run sequentially.
  - o **linear:** Tasks run sequentially, but Ansible waits for each host to complete before moving on to the next in a play.
  - o **Note:** Ansible offers more advanced strategies, but these are a great start.

Fact Gathering

Before running tasks, Ansible can collect information about your hosts called 'facts':

- **[defaults]**
  - o **gather_facts:** Controls whether facts are gathered automatically at the start of a play.
  - o **gather_subset:** Lets you narrow down which specific categories of facts to collect for greater efficiency.

Resource Optimization

When managing large swathes of infrastructure, these settings become vital:

- **[defaults]**
  - o **forks:** How many hosts to work on in parallel (Higher = faster, but consumes more resources).

- **poll_interval:** Time Ansible waits between checks on long-running tasks.

Additional Resources

- **Mastering Ansible Configuration Settings:** https://docs.ansible.com/ansible/latest/reference_appendices/config.html
- **Becoming Privileged (Sudo, Su, etc.):** https://docs.ansible.com/ansible/latest/user_guide/become.html
- **Ansible Execution Strategies:** https://docs.ansible.com/ansible/latest/user_guide/playbooks_strategies.html

Beyond the Basics

Let me emphasize that `ansible.cfg` offers far more settings than we can cover in these introductory chapters. View the official docs as your ultimate reference guide. For now, we've given you the tools to fine-tune how Ansible connects to hosts, gains the right permissions, and optimizes resource usage.

Coming Up Next

With a solid understanding of configuration, we're ready to move into the fascinating world of YAML – the language you'll use to describe the *what* of your Ansible automation.

Demystifying YAML: A Comprehensive Dive, Part 1

Get ready to embark on a journey into the heart of Ansible's instructions: the wonderfully structured world of YAML. Don't let the acronym (YAML Ain't Markup Language) mislead you. YAML is all about making your Ansible journey smooth by providing a human-readable way to describe your desired system states.

Why YAML?

- **Readability:** YAML focuses on being visually clear and uncluttered – a welcome change from overly complex configuration formats.
- **No programming required:** You don't need to be a programmer to grasp its structure.
- **Data-Oriented:** YAML excels at representing the kind of data you'll need for managing infrastructure (lists of servers, software packages, etc.).

The Fundamentals of Structure

YAML relies on two primary building blocks:

1. **Scalars (Key-Value Pairs):** Think of these as the most basic units. A key (on the left) is followed by a colon and its corresponding value.

    Example:

    ```
    server_name: webserver01
    os_version:  Ubuntu 22.04
    ```

2. **Lists:** Sequences of items. Denoted a few ways:
    - ➢ `-` prefix for each item:

```
tasks:
  - name: Install Apache webserver
    package: apache2
```

> Square brackets [ ]:

```
database_servers: [db01.example.com, db02.example.com]
```

Maps (a.k.a Dictionaries or Hashes)

These let you group related key-value pairs to represent more complex objects. A map starts at an indentation level and each key-value pair sits on a new line below:

```
webserver:
  hostname: web01.example.com
  ip_address: 192.168.1.50
  software:
    - apache2
    - php
```

Indentation Matters!

Unlike some languages, YAML uses whitespace (indentation) to define its structure. Be consistent! A common standard is to use two spaces per indentation level. Sloppy spacing will make YAML angry.

Comments

Start a line with # to add explanations right within your YAML.

```
# Install the necessary network monitoring packages
```

```yaml
- name: Install SNMP tools
  package:
    name: net-snmp
    state: present
```

Additional Resources

- **YAML Official Website:** https://yaml.org/
- **Learn X in Y Minutes: YAML** (For a quick refresher):https://learnxinyminutes.com/docs/yaml/

Coming Up Next

In Part 2, we'll delve into advanced YAML features like multi-line values, merging data structures, and explore where YAML fits in your Ansible Playbooks.

Tip: The best way to master YAML is to practice. The hands-on exercise in the next chapter will give you exactly that opportunity!

Unraveling the Mysteries of YAML: Deep Dive, Part 2

In the previous chapter, we explored the foundational building blocks of YAML. Now, let's unlock some more advanced techniques to give you even greater control over your Ansible automation.

Strings: Handling Text

- **Multi-line Strings:** Sometimes your data needs to span multiple lines. YAML offers a few ways:
    - **Folding (>):** Great for text paragraphs, preserves newlines.

        ```
        description: >
          This is a long description that
          will keep its formatting and
          line breaks.
        ```

    - **Literal (|):** Use this when you need to include newlines verbatim.
- **Quotes or No Quotes?:** YAML is flexible. You can use quotes around strings, but they're usually not necessary unless your string contains special characters or looks like another data type.

Data Merging: Combining Structures

Imagine you need to define default settings but allow overriding them for specific environments. YAML's 'merge' symbol (<<) to the rescue:

```
# defaults.yaml
common_packages:
```

```
  - nano
  - curl
  - wget

# production.yaml
web_servers:
  <<: *common_packages   # Merge!
  - apache2
```

YAML in Ansible Playbooks

So far, we looked at standalone YAML. When used in Ansible playbooks, a few key points:

- **Playbook Structure:** Playbooks are themselves big YAML files, with top-level elements like `hosts`, `tasks`, `vars`, etc.
- **Data within Tasks:** The modules you'll use in Ansible tasks (e.g., 'package', 'file') often take key-value parameters that form little YAML structures inside your playbook.

Advanced Concepts (A Peek)

Don't worry about grasping these fully now, they'll get their own chapters later. But, here's a taste to spark your curiosity:

- **Anchors & Aliases (& and * symbols):** Let you reuse YAML blocks to avoid repetition.
- **Flow Style:** Allows compactly writing lists and maps inline using brackets [ ] and braces { }.

Additional Resources

- **Advanced YAML Features:** Dig into YAML's official spec if you're feeling adventurous: https://yaml.org/spec/1.2.2/

Caution: With increased power comes increased responsibility. Incorrect YAML structure will lead to Ansible errors. Pay careful attention to detail.

Hands-On Exercise: Crafting YAML Wonders

It's time to roll up your sleeves and put the power of YAML into practice! In this exercise, we'll tackle real-world scenarios and solidify your understanding of this essential data language for Ansible.

Prerequisites

- **A Text Editor:** Choose your favorite (VS Code, Atom, Sublime Text, even a simple one like Notepad++ works)
- **Ansible Control Machine:** Remember, this is the computer where you'll install Ansible and create your exercise files.
- **A Sprinkle of Curiosity:** This journey is more fun when you're not afraid to experiment!

Exercise Scenario: Inventory Building Blocks

Imagine you're starting to manage a small infrastructure: 2 web servers, a database server, and a monitoring server. Your first task is to map this out in YAML format, which will form the basis of your future Ansible playbooks.

Tasks

1. **Structuring the Basics:**
    - Create a file named `inventory.yml`.
    - Define the following groups of hosts: 'webservers', 'databases', and 'monitoring'.
    - Place appropriate server hostnames or IP addresses under each group. Since this is an exercise, you can invent some if you don't have real servers readily available. (e.g., web01.example.com, db01.example.com, etc.)

2. **Variables for Flexibility:**
    - At the top of your file, define an Ansible variable named `apache_version` and set it to the latest Apache package version you can find online.
    - Consider adding another variable to represent a common software package (e.g., 'ntp' for a time synchronization service) that you would install on all your servers.
3. **Group-level Variables:** Think about a setting that might be specific to your database servers. Perhaps a backup location? Create a YAML dictionary under the `databases` group and define a variable called `backup_path` with a suitable value.

Example (Partial)

```yaml
---
apache_version: '2.4.54'   # Example - Find the latest!

webservers:
  - web01.example.com
  - web02.example.com

databases:
  - db01.example.com
  backup_path: '/backups/databases'
```

Tips

- **Comments are King:** Use # to explain your thought process and choices within the YAML.
- **Validate!** As you get more advanced, there are YAML linting tools, but for now, checking your indentation carefully is key to avoid errors.

- **Ansible Inventory Docs as a Guide:** You'll dive deeper into Ansible Inventory in upcoming chapters, but for handy reference: https://docs.ansible.com/ansible/latest/user_guide/intro_inventory.html]

Bonus Challenges (If you feel adventurous)

- **Nested Groups:** Can you create a top-level group called 'production' and nest your existing groups under it?
- **More Variables:** Explore how variable precedence works in Ansible. Introduce a variable at the play level (top of the file) with the same name as one of your group variables. What would happen?

Remember, this isn't just about the YAML syntax; it's about starting to visualize how your Ansible automation will map to the real-world infrastructure you want to manage!

Section 3:
Mapping Your Territory: Ansible Inventory

Crafting Your Ansible Arsenal: Understanding Inventory

Think of your Ansible inventory as a grand map guiding your automation adventures. An effective inventory is essential for pinpointing exactly which servers you want to target with your playbooks and how Ansible should connect to them.

The Heart of It All: The Inventory File

Your inventory file (traditionally `hosts` or `inventory.ini` or `.yml`) serves as the primary source for Ansible, although more dynamic sources are possible (we'll touch on those later). Typically, you'll have at least one of these files. Let's break down its core concepts:

- **Hosts:** The most basic unit. A host can be a hostname (https://example.com/hostname) or an IP address.
- **Groups:** The key to organization. Group hosts logically by function (webservers), environment (production), location… whatever makes sense for *your* infrastructure.
- **Variables:** You can attach variables to individual hosts *or* entire groups, giving you flexibility in defining connection

details, software versions, or other settings specific to targets.

Default Inventory Location

Ansible will look for your inventory in several places:

- The current working directory.
- `/etc/ansible/hosts` (configured in `ansible.cfg`).
- You can override this via the `-i` flag to the `ansible` or `ansible-playbook` commands.

Static vs. Dynamic Inventories

- **Static Inventories:** Perfect for smaller setups or those that don't change frequently. You define hosts and groups directly in the file.
- **Dynamic Inventories:** Awesome for environments where your servers are constantly added, removed, or sourced from cloud providers (AWS, Azure, etc.). Dynamic inventories are scripts or plugins that fetch your list of hosts on the fly during playbook execution.

Additional Resources

- **Ansible Inventory Introduction:** https://docs.ansible.com/ansible/latest/user_guide/intro_inventory.html
- **Working with Dynamic Inventory:** https://docs.ansible.com/ansible/latest/user_guide/intro_dynamic_inventory.html

Beyond the Basics

Let's highlight a few important concepts that will unlock Ansible's inventory potential:

- **Patterns:** Use host patterns to select multiple hosts at once (e.g., `webservers[01:20]`). Great for large sets of similar servers.
- **Aliases:** Define alternative names for hosts, especially useful for long server names. Makes your playbooks more readable.
- **Nested Groups & Child Groups:** Create hierarchies for complex environments. A group of 'database' servers could be nested under a broader group called 'backend.'
- **Variables at Every Level:** You can set variables at the host, group, or even playbook level. Understanding how these combine requires a touch of finesse that we'll dedicate an entire chapter to.

Inventory Best Practices

1. **Clarity is King:** Choose meaningful names for groups and hosts that align with how *you* think about your infrastructure.
2. **Embrace Variables:** Use them smartly to minimize repetition and make changes easy.
3. **Start Simple, Grow Smartly:** Even complex inventories start as simple lists.
4. **Version Control:** If you use a tool like Git to track your playbook changes, include your inventory as well! This enables you to track how your infrastructure has evolved over time.

Up Next

Get ready for a hands-on exercise where you'll build your own inventory file, experiment with grouping, and get familiar with attaching variables.

Practical Exercise: Crafting Your Inventory Arsenal

It's time to translate inventory concepts into practice! In this exercise, we'll create a well-structured inventory file and experiment with managing a realistic (but scaled down) infrastructure.

Prerequisites

- **Ansible Control Machine**
- **Text Editor**
- **Inventory file** (If you didn't build on in the previous YAML exercise, start with a fresh `inventory.yml` file)

Scenario: Mapping a Multi-Tier Application

Imagine you're managing a classic 3-tier web application setup:

- **Web Frontends:** 3 servers: `web01.example.com`, `web02.example.com`, `web03.example.com`
- **Application Servers:** 2 servers: `app01.example.com`, `app02.example.com`
- **Database Backend:** 1 server `db01.example.com`

Tasks

1. **Structuring the Inventory**
    - Create groups in your inventory file for 'webservers', 'appservers', and 'databases'.
    - Place the appropriate hostnames or IPs under each group.
2. **Common Variables**

- At the top of your file, introduce a few variables that would likely apply to all of your servers:
    - `ansible_user`: The username Ansible will use to connect.
    - `ansible_port`: If you're using a non-standard SSH port.
3. **Group-Specific Settings**
    - Under the 'webservers' group, add a variable called `max_http_clients` and set a suitable value.
    - Experiment with nesting! Create a 'prod' group and place your 'webservers', 'appservers', and 'databases' groups within it, signifying your production environment.
4. **Test Connection with Ansible**
    - Type: `ansible all -m ping` (This should reach all hosts in your inventory if connectivity is set up correctly)
    - Try targeting a specific group: `ansible webservers -m ping`

Example: (Partial)

```yaml
---
ansible_user: devops_user
ansible_port: 22

prod:
  children:
    webservers:
      hosts:
        web01.example.com:
        web02.example.com:
        web03.example.com:
      vars:
        max_http_clients: 200
```

```
    appservers:
      hosts:
        # ... add your appservers here
    databases:
      hosts:
        # ... add your database server here
```

Tips

- **Leverage Comments:** Explain your design choices using # in your inventory file.
- **Experiment:** Try adding variables at different levels (host, group). Observe how Ansible might determine which value "wins" if there are conflicts.
- **Documentation is Your Friend:** Revisit the Ansible Inventory docs for syntax if needed: https://docs.ansible.com/ansible/latest/user_guide/intro_inventory.html

Bonus Challenges (Feeling Adventurous?)

- **Host Patterns:** Modify your `ansible all -m ping` command to use a host pattern, targeting all production servers whose hostnames end in '01'.
- **Research:** How could you use a **dynamic inventory** script with Ansible to pull your host list directly from a cloud provider like AWS?

Key Takeaway: A well-crafted inventory is the foundation upon which your Ansible playbooks will execute. Putting time into thoughtfully organizing it now will save you tons of headaches later!

Inventory Alchemy: Exploring Formats and Structures

In previous chapters, we built a solid foundation for our Ansible inventory. It's time to level up! Let's transform your inventory from a simple list into a powerful tool using different formats, clever organization, and even injecting data from external sources.

Beyond INI and YAML

While the INI-like format (`.ini`) or YAML (`.yml`) are Ansible's most common inventory file formats, it's good to know that Ansible supports several others:

- **JSON:** If you're already using JSON to structure data elsewhere in your environment, Ansible can work with that too.
- **Executable Scripts:** For truly dynamic scenarios, where your list of hosts needs to be generated at runtime, you can write executable scripts in Python, Perl, etc.
- **Cloud Inventory Sources:** Ansible has plugins for many cloud providers (AWS, Azure, GCP, DigitalOcean, etc.), letting you dynamically fetch your server lists.

Structuring with Directory Hierarchies

For larger infrastructures, you can split your inventory across multiple files and directories. Consider this example structure:

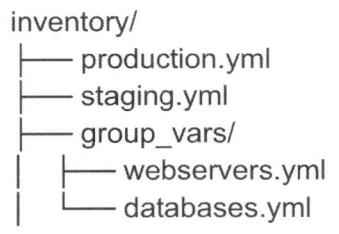

```
inventory/
├── production.yml
├── staging.yml
├── group_vars/
│   ├── webservers.yml
│   └── databases.yml
```

```
└── host_vars/
    ├── web01.example.com.yml
    └── db01.example.com.yml
```

Observations:

- **Environments:** Separate inventories for production, testing, etc.
- **group_vars:** Files containing variables specific to a group.
- **host_vars:** Files to hold variables for individual hosts.

Important: Ansible has rules for how it merges data when you have this type of setup. Variables at more specific levels take precedence.

External Data Sources

What if you already have a database or a configuration management tool (CMDB) that stores your server information? Here are a few ways to leverage that:

- **Script-Based Dynamic Inventories:** Write scripts to query your data source and output an Ansible-compatible JSON list of hosts.
- **Custom Inventory Plugins:** For complex integrations, you can get more sophisticated by developing custom inventory plugins for Ansible (a bit more advanced).

Additional Resources

- **Inventory Formats (Official Docs):** https://docs.ansible.com/ansible/latest/user_guide/intro_inventory.html#inventory-formats
- **Working with Dynamic Inventory:** https://docs.ansible.com/ansible/latest/user_guide/intro_dynamic_inventory.html

Security Considerations

Your inventory might contain sensitive information like connection details, passwords (if stored as variables), and more.

- **Limit Access:** Ensure only authorized users can access your inventory files using file permissions.
- **Ansible Vault:** For secrets, use Ansible Vault to encrypt sensitive data within your inventory or related variable files.

Up Next: Grouping and Hierarchies

In the next chapter, we'll dive deeper into creating powerful hierarchies within your inventory to streamline your Ansible automation tasks.

Forging Alliances: Grouping and Hierarchies in Inventory Management

Just as a powerful army has regiments, divisions, and a clear chain of command, a well-structured Ansible inventory will greatly enhance your automation expeditions. In this chapter, we'll focus on grouping strategies and creating hierarchies to target your hosts with laser precision.

The Power of Groups

Here's why effective grouping is your Ansible superpower:

- **Focused Actions:** Groups let you run tasks on specific slices of your infrastructure (`ansible webservers -m service -a "name=httpd state=restarted"`).
- **Variable Targeting:** Assign variables tailored to each group's needs (webservers might have different memory limits than backend database servers).
- **Organization & Understanding:** Well-named groups make both your inventory and the intentions of your playbooks more human-readable.

Simple Grouping

You've seen the basics – defining groups in your inventory file:

```
[webservers]
web01.example.com
web02.example.com

[databases]
db01.example.com
```

Groups of Groups: Nesting for the Win

To model more complex environments, groups can contain other groups!

```
[production]    # A top-level group

  [webservers:children]   # 'children' keyword is key
    web01.example.com
    web02.example.com

  [databases:children]
    db01.example.com
```

- **Targeting Tip:** Ansible commands target all hosts within a parent group and its child groups.

Patterns: Wielding Wildcards

Use wildcard-like patterns to select hosts for groups or target matching hosts for ad-hoc tasks:

- `[frontend:1:5].example.com` — Matches frontend01 through frontend05
- `[dbservers:vars]` - Creates a group of any hosts that have the 'dbserver' substring anywhere in their name (use with caution!)

Implicit Groups: Based on Facts

Ansible automatically creates some groups based on 'facts' gathered about your hosts:

- `ungrouped`: If a host doesn't belong to any defined groups

- `all`: Targets all your managed hosts
- OS-based groups: `linux`, `windows`
- And many more based on discovered properties

Additional Resources

- **Inventory Patterns:**
  https://docs.ansible.com/ansible/latest/user_guide/intro_patterns.html
- **Smart Group Creation with Facts:**
  https://docs.ansible.com/ansible/latest/user_guide/intro_dynamic_inventory.html#smart-group-creation-with-facts

Organizing Variables with Hierarchies

Remember, you can attach variables at host, group, or even the top level (affecting all hosts). Consider:

```
# Common to ALL hosts:
ansible_port: 22

[webservers]
http_port: 80

[databases]
db_backup_enabled: true
```

The Art of the Override

If the same variable is defined more specifically, it overrides more general values (precedence rules are covered in a dedicated chapter!). This lets you set sane defaults while customizing specific groups or hosts.

Section 4:
Harnessing the Power of Ansible Variables

Unleashing the Magic of Ansible Variables

Imagine variables as containers that hold information you want to reuse throughout your Ansible journey. They are the key to making your playbooks adaptable and reducing repetitive hardcoding. In this chapter, we'll explore their superpowers and different flavors!

Why Variables Rock

- **Flexibility:** Use a variable for a software version, and it becomes trivial to update that version everywhere it's used across your playbooks and inventory.
- **Data-Driven Decisions:** Let variables hold information gathered from your servers (like operating system type) and change your playbook's behavior accordingly.
- **Clarity:** Well-named variables make your Ansible code far easier to read and understand than raw values littered throughout.

Where to Define Variables

Ansible lets you define variables at various places:

1. **Inventory:** Your inventory file (`hosts`, INI-style, or YAML) can hold variables at the individual host level or for entire groups.
2. **Playbooks:** Variables defined within your playbooks, usually towards the top.
3. **Variable Files:** Separate `.yaml` files dedicated to variables (often alongside your inventory or grouped within dedicated folders).
4. **Command Line:** Use the `-e` (or `--extra-vars`) flag when running Ansible commands to pass in variables.

Example: Setting a Package Name

```
---
- hosts: webservers
  vars:
    webserver_package: apache2   # Playbook level variable
  tasks:
    - name: Install webserver
      package:
        name: "{{ webserver_package }}"   # Using the variable
        state: latest
```

Types of Variables

- **User-Defined:** The ones you create yourself for customization – they have no inherent special meaning to Ansible.
- **Facts:** Ansible gathers *facts* about your hosts – OS, memory, etc. These are like built-in variables.
- **Magic Variables:** Ansible gives you special values to use for things like the current playbook, connection information, and more.

Additional Resources

- **Ansible Variable Docs:** Get comfortable with the official reference: https://docs.ansible.com/ansible/latest/user_guide/playbooks_variables.html

Best Practices

1. **Descriptive Names:** `apache_version` is better than `x`.
2. **Organization:** Inventory is good for server groups, use variable files for complex structures.
3. **Avoid Overkill:** Super simple tasks might not *need* variables, but it's a good habit to build.

Up Next

We're about to go deeper! Next, we'll discuss different ways you can *source* variables, from simple defaults to more dynamic methods.

Deciphering Variable Varieties

In the previous chapter, we saw how variables become the building blocks of your Ansible playbooks. Now, prepare to unlock a whole arsenal of techniques for defining and sourcing them, giving you precise control over how they shape your automation.

Types of User-Defined Variables

Let's break down the most common ways you'll likely be creating your own variables to use within Ansible:

- **Simple Values:** For strings, numbers, or true/false:

    ```
    max_requests: 250
    os_family: 'Debian'
    enable_firewall: true
    ```

- **Lists (Arrays):** Great for ordered sequences:

    ```
    backup_directories:
      - /etc
      - /home
      - /var/log
    ```

- **Dictionaries (Hashes):** When you need key-value pairings:

    ```
    database_config:
      host: db01.example.com
      port: 3306
      username: webapp
    ```

Where and When: A Recap

Recall where you can inject your variables:

- **Inventory:** Host and group-level variables.
- **Playbooks:** Variables at the top level or within tasks.
- **Variable Files:** Standalone `.yaml` files (include them in playbooks).
- **Command Line (-e flag):** For on-the-fly adjustments during playbook runs.

Fact Gathering: Ansible's Secret Weapon

- **Automatic:** When you run playbooks, Ansible collects *facts* about your target hosts.
- **Use Them Anywhere:** Access facts like a variable: `{{ ansible_distribution }}`, `{{ ansible_hostname }}`, etc.

Registering Variables: Capturing Results

Think of this as storing the results of a task so you can utilize them later.

Example:

```
- name: Get installed version of Apache
  package_facts:
    manager: apt

- name: Store the version
  register: apache_version_data

- name: Print the version if it exists
  debug:
    var: apache_version_data.ansible_facts.packages.apache2[0].version
```

Additional Resources

- **Facts: The Reference:** The "setup" module gathers facts – see the full list! https://docs.ansible.com/ansible/latest/collections/ansible/builtin/setup_module.html]

Caution: Scope Matters

Remember where you define a variable determines where it's accessible. A variable defined in a play won't be visible to a task running on a different host.

Up Next: Precedence Battles

You might define the same variable in multiple places. In the next chapter, we'll uncover the rules Ansible uses to decide which value wins – Variable Precedence!

Capturing Triumphs: Variable Registration and Precedence, Unveiled, Part 1

Imagine a grand Ansible cook-off where multiple chefs (playbooks, inventory, etc.) contribute ingredients (variables), but only one version of each dish (value) can make it to the plate! Precedence rules are the head judge determining whose recipe wins.

Why Precedence Matters

- **Flexibility:** Define the same variable at different levels for customizing behavior.
- **Overrides:** Provide defaults, but let specific scenarios take control if needed.
- **Troubleshooting:** Key to understanding why Ansible used a certain value, helping you debug.

The Basic Idea: Specificity Wins

Generally, the more *specific* the place you define a variable, the higher its precedence:

1. **Role Defaults:** (Lowest) The least specific – think of these as baseline settings.
2. **Inventory (Group & Host Vars):** Overrides defaults if set for groups your hosts belong to.
3. **Playbook Vars:** Values within the playbook itself generally take priority.
4. **Facts:** Facts about the system gathered by Ansible can hold high precedence.
5. **Registered Variables:** Capturing task output unlocks extra power.
6. **Command Line (-e):** (Highest) Overrides for one-off runs.

Example: Let's Battle for Web Server Port!

- **Inventory Group Variable:** `webserver_port: 80`
- **Playbook Variable:** `webserver_port: 8080`
- **Task:**

```
- name: Install Apache Web Server
  package:
    name: apache2
    state: present
  register: apache_install_result
```

Who Wins? The playbook variable! This ensures any play-specific port setting takes over inventory values.

But Wait, There's More!

- Ansible has a whopping 16+ levels of precedence (it's detailed in the docs!).
- Some types of variables are 'extra vars' and have special placement in the order.
- This is the *general* idea – certain variables related to Ansible's internal workings can break this pattern.

Additional Resources

- **Behold, the Full Precedence Table:** Warning, it's a bit overwhelming for beginners! https://docs.ansible.com/ansible/latest/user_guide/playbooks_variables.html#variable-precedence-where-should-i-put-a-variable

Up Next: Part 2

In the next part, we'll use scenarios to illustrate these concepts and introduce some of the nuances within precedence levels themselves.

Capturing Triumphs: Variable Registration and Precedence, Unveiled, Part 2

In the previous chapter, we began exploring how Ansible decides which variable to use when conflicts arise. Let's tackle some more scenarios to solidify this knowledge!

Scenario 1: Facts in the Ring

Facts Ansible gathers about your system can have surprisingly high precedence. Imagine this in your inventory:

```
[webservers]
webserver_port: 8080
```

But, a task reveals the OS is Debian-based with Apache already on port 80:

```
- name: Get Apache information
  package_facts:
    manager: apt
  register: installed_packages
```

If you reference `{{ ansible_distribution_version }}` or `{{ installed_packages }}` within your tasks targeting "webservers", facts will likely override your inventory. Ansible prioritizes the *current state* of the system.

Scenario 2: Vars within Vars

You can have variables reference... other variables!

```
webserver_base_port: 80
```

```
http_port: "{{ webserver_base_port }}{{ webserver_suffix }}"
```

- **Precedence within the Variable:** It resolves the *inner* part first (if `webserver_suffix` was set somewhere, otherwise, it defaults to an empty string).
- **Overall Precedence:** Still follows the standard rules – a playbook-level `http_port` would win.

Special Case: 'extra-vars' (-e flag)

Variables passed from the command line hold supreme power. They're designed for temporary overrides during testing, not as your primary way of managing variables.

Example:

```
ansible-playbook my_playbook.yml -e "database_backup_enabled=false"
```

Debugging Tip

Use Ansible's debug module to print the value of a variable mid-playbook:

```
- name: Show me the current value of the port
  debug:
```

```
var: webserver_port
```

Additional Notes

- A few niche situations can break the typical precedence order. Remember, the docs are the ultimate source of truth for those complex cases!
- Best practice is to be predictable. Strive for a clear structure of where you set variables, so you (and future you!) can understand your own Ansible logic more easily.

Scoping Out Variable Terrain

Think of your Ansible expedition as venturing across different regions of configuration. Variables, like supplies, have limited reach. Understanding their scope empowers you to pack the right tools for each stage of your journey!

Scope Levels

1. **Global Scope:**
    - Defined in: Ansible configuration files (e.g., `ansible.cfg`).
    - Reach: Everywhere within your Ansible project.
    - Rarely used directly by beginners – usually for Ansible's own behavior, not your tasks.
2. **Playbook Scope:**
    - Defined in: At the top of your playbooks (the `vars` section).
    - Reach: Available to all tasks within that specific playbook.
3. **Task Scope:**
    - Defined in: Directly within a task using `vars`.
    - Reach: Limited to that individual task.
    - Perfect for temporary variables used only for a single step.
4. **Host/Group Variables (Inventory Scope):**
    - Defined in: Your inventory file, attached to specific groups or individual hosts.
    - Reach: Accessible only when Ansible is targeting hosts they're associated with.

Scope in Action: Setting a Backup Path

- **Global:** Rarely for user data, but maybe a path prefix for *all* backups if your Ansible setup backs up multiple projects.

- **Playbook:** `backup_base_dir: '/backups'` if the entire playbook backs up a single service to the same location.
- **Host:** In inventory, 'node1_backup_dir' and 'node2_backup_dir' for servers holding different datasets.
- **Task:** A temp variable if just one task calculates a subdirectory based on today's date.

Visibility: When Can You See It?

A variable's scope determines where you can *use* it, not just where you define it. A play-level variable is useless if the task runs on a host that's not targeted by that play!

Tip: Playbooks Target Hosts

Remember, your playbook has a `hosts` key. Tasks work on that subset of your inventory, thus only variables associated with those hosts, or those with broader scope, matter to that task.

Additional Resources

- **Docs on Variable Scopes:** (Feels a bit dry, but it's a good reference when things get complex!) https://docs.ansible.com/ansible/latest/user_guide/playbooks_variables.html#variable-scopes

Pro Tip: Be Mindful of Scope Override

It's tempting to re-use variable names. A task-level `http_port` won't *break* things but can cause confusion and unintended overriding of values defined elsewhere.

Up Next: Magic Variables

Ansible gives you a special toolkit of built-in 'magic' variables revealing information about the current playbook, host, and more!

Peering into the Mystical Realm: Ansible's Magic Variables

Ansible secretly weaves 'magic variables' into the fabric of your playbooks. Unlike the ones you create, these provide dynamic information about your hosts, the playbook itself, and more. Think of them as enchanted compasses guiding your automation journey!

Types of Magic

Let's explore a few of the most commonly useful categories:

- **Host-Specific Facts:** Access any fact Ansible discovered!
    - `ansible_hostname`: The hostname.
    - `ansible_os_family`: "Debian", "RedHat", etc.
    - `ansible_distribution_version`: OS version.
    - *Tip:* Use `ansible somehost -m setup` to see *all* facts for a host!
- **Inventory Insights:**
    - `hostvars`: Access another host's variables (`hostvars['web01']['http_port']`)
    - `group_names`: A list of groups the current host belongs to.
    - `groups`: All groups in your inventory with their hosts.
- **Playbook Power:**
    - `playbook_dir`: The directory containing your current playbook – great if your playbooks reference supporting files.
    - `inventory_hostname` – Short name of the host Ansible is working on.

Putting Magic to Use

1. **Conditional Logic:**

   ```
   - name: Install Apache if Debian-based
     package:
       name: apache2
       state: present
     when: ansible_os_family == 'Debian'
   ```

2. **Templating:** (Wait for the chapters on templating!)

   ```
   - name: Create a config file tailored to the OS
     template:
       src: my_app.conf.j2   # .j2 is for Jinja2 templating
       dest: /etc/my_app/config.conf
     notify: restart my_app  # You'll learn about handlers soon!
   ```

3. **Debugging:**

   ```
   - name: Print the full list of packages installed
     debug:
       msg: "{{ ansible_facts['packages'] }}"
   ```

Words of Caution

- **Avoid Overreliance:** While powerful, too much reliance on magic variables can make playbooks harder to understand for others (or future you!)
- **Fact Gathering Overhead:** Some facts can be slow to gather, especially on large numbers of hosts.

Additional Resources

- **The Vault of Magic:** The Ansible docs list many magic variables, but don't feel overwhelmed!

https://docs.ansible.com/ansible/latest/reference_appendices/special_variables.html

Up Next: Facts – Ansible's Crystal Ball

In the next chapter, we'll dive deeper into Ansible Facts. Get ready to harness information about your systems to make your playbooks even more adaptable!

The Saga of Ansible Facts Unfolded

Imagine Ansible as a brave knight on a quest to manage your infrastructure. Facts are the detailed reports its trusty scouts send back from each castle (server) in your kingdom. These facts reveal everything from the castle's operating system (its ruling dynasty) to the supplies within (installed software).

Ansible's Fact-Finding Mission

By default, at the start of every playbook targeting a host, Ansible embarks on a 'setup' task. This isn't visible in your playbook code but think of it as these scouts doing the following:

- **Hardware Recon:** Memory, CPU cores, network devices... understanding the castle's strength.
- **OS Intel:** Linux, Windows, its version... the laws of the land the castle follows.
- **Inventory Time:** List of all installed packages (software), versions... every treasure or tool inside.
- **And More!** IP addresses, filesystems, even custom facts you can define.

Why Facts Are Your Secret Weapon

Facts make your Ansible playbooks intelligent:

1. **Decisions, Decisions:**

```
- name: Install the right web server package
  package:
    name: "{{ 'apache2' if ansible_os_family == 'Debian' else 'httpd' }}"
    state: present
```

2. **Inventory Insights:** Let's say you store a database password per-host in your inventory. You can reference another host's fact to connect to it.
3. **Debugging:** If something breaks, seeing the exact state Ansible "saw" on the target machine helps you pinpoint the issue.

Accessing Your Facts

Ansible facts are like variables: `ansible_distribution`, `ansible_memory_mb.real.total`, etc. But, you don't define them, Ansible does the hard work!

Important Notes

- **Fact Gathering Takes Time:** In large setups, it can add overhead. Use `gather_facts: false` at the play level to skip it if you don't need the facts.
- **Security:** Facts might reveal sensitive info. Ansible Vault can encrypt them.
- **Custom Facts:** You can write scripts for Ansible to gather specialized info.

Additional Resources

- **Behold, The List:** Be prepared, it's long! This is where you see the full range of default facts Ansible gathers: https://docs.ansible.com/ansible/latest/user_guide/playbooks_vars_facts.html#ansible-standard-facts

Time to Exercise Your Fact Power!

Next, a hands-on exploration of using facts within your playbooks is essential. Try building tasks that react differently based on operating systems or available memory!

Practical Application: Variable Mastery and Fact Finding Expedition

It's time to embark on a true Ansible quest! We'll arm ourselves with variables, harness the wisdom of facts, and tackle practical infrastructure management challenges. Remember, this expedition is as much about the journey as the destination.

Scenario: Deploying a Multi-Tier Website

Let's imagine deploying a website with these components:

- **Frontend Web Servers:** (group: 'webservers') – Serving HTML, CSS, JavaScript to users.
- **Backend Application Servers:** (group: 'appservers') – Running a Python/Flask application.
- **Database Server:** (group: 'database') – Holding website data.

Expedition Goals

1. **Software Consistency:** Install the right web server (Apache or Nginx) and database software (e.g., PostgreSQL) based on the operating system of each server group.
2. **Customization:** Accept a version number as an input when running our playbook, so we can update components easily.
3. **Security:** Reference a database password stored securely within our Ansible inventory.

Pre-Expedition Prep

- **Basic Inventory:** Set up your `hosts` file (or dynamic inventory) with the servers under the groups mentioned above.
- **Ansible Playbook Outline:** Start a `site_setup.yml` playbook, it can be simple for now:

```yaml
---
- hosts: all
  gather_facts: true # We'll need Facts!
  vars:
    # ... Our variables will be added here ...

  tasks:
    ## ... And the tasks to achieve our goals will go here ...
```

Quest Stages

1. **OS-aware Installations:**
   - Define variables like `webserver_package` and `database_package` at the playbook level.
   - Use when conditionals with `ansible_os_family` in tasks to install the right packages.
2. **Version Control:**
   - Introduce a variable like `app_version`.
   - Utilize command-line `-e` during playbook runs for now (e.g., `ansible-playbook site_setup.yml -e "app_version=1.2.0"`).
3. **Secure the Database Password**
   - Add an encrypted `db_password` variable in your inventory (Ansible Vault is beyond the scope of this chapter, but note its importance!).
   - Modify a database setup task to reference `{{ db_password }}`.

Tips

- **Small Steps:** Break tasks down. Test installing *just* the web server first!
- **Embrace the Debug Module:** Use `debug: msg: "{{ ansible_memtotal_mb }}"` to peek at facts during runs.
- **Document:** Add comments to your playbook explaining your variable choices and logic.

Beyond the Basics (Teasers for Future Chapters)

- **Variable Precedence Battles:** Purposely introduce conflicts and observe how Ansible resolves them.
- **Templating:** Create a configuration file template (`my_app.conf.j2`) and use variables within it!

Section 5: Orchestrating with Ansible Playbooks

Crafting the Symphony: Introduction to Ansible Playbooks

If variables are the instruments and Ansible's inventory is your orchestra, then playbooks are the sheet music that brings your automation to life. In this chapter, we'll learn the fundamentals of composing playbooks that will conduct your systems in perfect harmony.

The Essence of a Playbook

At their heart, Ansible playbooks are YAML files. They define the following:

- **Hosts:** One or more groups/hosts from your inventory that this playbook will target.
- **Tasks:** Ordered steps that Ansible should execute on those hosts.
- **Variables:** Customization for your playbook (you already know about these!).
- **More:** You'll soon learn about conditionals (when), loops, error handling… the full repertoire!

Anatomy of a Simple Playbook

Let's dissect a basic example:

```yaml
--- # Every playbook starts with this
- hosts: webservers
  become: true  # Often needed to run tasks with admin rights

  tasks:
    - name: Install Apache webserver
      package:
        name: httpd
        state: present

    - name: Ensure Apache is running
      service:
        name: httpd
        state: started
```

Observations

- **Playbooks are a List of Plays:** Technically, you can have multiple `- hosts:` sections for different stages, but beginners usually have one.
- **Indentation is King:** YAML cares about those spaces! Defines the structure.
- **Modules are Your Tools:** `package` and `service` are Ansible modules — they do the heavy lifting of managing software and services.

Running Your Playbook

Assuming the above is saved as `install_web.yml`, you'd use the `ansible-playbook` command:

```
ansible-playbook install_web.yml
```

Key Concepts

1. **Order Matters:** Tasks generally execute top to bottom (unless you start using fancy control flow later).
2. **Idempotence:** A fancy word meaning that Ansible aims to reach the *desired state*. If Apache is already installed, the package task effectively does nothing. This makes re-runs safe.
3. **Modules Are the Magic:** Ansible comes with *hundreds* of built-in ways to manage common system tasks – that's where the true power lies!

Additional Resources

- **Ansible Docs on Playbooks:** The official source for more details and options: https://docs.ansible.com/ansible/latest/user_guide/playbooks.html

Up Next: Playbook Checkup

We'll learn techniques to verify your playbooks execute as intended and explore ways to make sure they halt if something unexpected happens.

Fine-Tuning Your Harmony: Playbook Verification Techniques

Imagine Ansible playbooks as the blueprints for grand renovations of your infrastructure. Before sending in the construction crews (making actual changes!), you wouldn't just wing it, right? This chapter is about those safety checks and testing methods that'll save you tons of automation headaches.

Why Verification Matters

- **Confidence:** Ensure your playbooks do what you *think* they'll do. Prevent surprises!
- **Error Prevention:** Catch typos in variables, incorrect paths, or misunderstandings of how Ansible modules work early in the process.
- **Debugging Aid:** When things *do* go wrong on production systems, these techniques help you pinpoint the culprit.

1. Start with Dry Runs (--check)

Your most powerful tool is Ansible's "what if" mode:

```
ansible-playbook deploy_website.yml --check
```

- **No Changes:** Nothing is *actually* modified on your target servers.
- **Simulated Results:** Ansible shows you what it *would have done*, task by task.
- **Great for Early Development:** When playbooks are incomplete or you're unsure if they target the right hosts.

2. Lint Your Playbooks!

Ever heard of Ansible-lint? It's like a spellchecker and grammar guru for your playbooks:

- **Catches Syntax Errors:** Missing colons, bad YAML formatting, etc.
- **Enforces Best Practices:** Warns about common pitfalls that might not be errors *yet*, but could cause trouble later.

Think of `--check` as testing if your machine works, and linting as checking if you built the machine *right* in the first place.

3. Debugging Module Output

The debug module is your stethoscope:

```
- name: Show the currently configured timezone
  debug:
    var: ansible_date_time.tz
```

- **Peeking Inside:** Lets you print the value of variables, facts, or even complex data structures generated by other modules.
- **Troubleshooting's Best Friend:** When a task fails mysteriously, seeing *why* an Ansible condition failed is invaluable.

4. Limit Your Focus (`--start-at-task`)

- **Big Playbooks:** Don't rerun everything from the beginning each time!
- **Syntax Issues Fixed:** Jump to the task you were working on with `ansible-playbook deploy.yml --start-at-task="Install database server"`

5. Stepping Through Playbooks (`--step`)

- **Forced Pause:** Ansible asks you if it should proceed to the next task.
- **Ideal for Risky Changes:** Or, if you need to inspect the system manually mid-playbook.

Additional Resources

- **Ansible-lint Rules:** The full list of things it can warn you about: https://github.com/ansible-community/ansible-lint/blob/main/docs/rules/index.rst

Tuning In to Quality: Ansible-lint for Playbook Perfection

Ansible-lint is like an automated music critic for your playbooks, pointing out sloppy rhythms and disharmonious notes. By catching mistakes *before* they hit the production stage, it saves you from embarrassing (and potentially disruptive) automation blunders.

Why Ansible-lint Is Your Friend

1. **Best Practices Beacon:** It nudges you towards writing playbooks the 'Ansible way,' making them easier for others (and future-you) to understand.
2. **Consistency Enforcer:** Ensures you follow your own naming conventions, making large playbooks more manageable.
3. **Potential Disaster Detector:** It can find things like using deprecated modules or risky configurations you might've overlooked.

Installing Ansible-lint

Usually, this is a simple `pip install ansible-lint`. Distribution-specific package managers might also have it. **Refer to the Ansible-lint docs for the most up-to-date instructions.**

Linting Your First Playbook

Let's say you have a playbook called `site_update.yml`. You'd run:

```
ansible-lint site_update.yml
```

Understanding the Output

Ansible-lint tags each issue it finds with a specific rule name and a short explanation. Some warnings are merely style suggestions, while others highlight potential errors.

Common Types of Lint Warnings

- **Indentation Trouble:** YAML is picky, Ansible-lint makes sure you've got your spacing right.
- **Unused Variables:** Suggests cleanup to avoid confusion.
- **Risky Module Options:** Warns about module settings that could have unintended side-effects.
- **Outdated Practices:** Points out if you're using modules or syntax in a deprecated way.
- **And Many More!:** Rules cover naming conventions, security, task best practices…

Customizing the Rules

You can disable overly strict rules, or even write your own if your organization has specific standards. Ansible-lint is flexible!

Additional Resources

- **The Rulebook:** See the full list of checks Ansible-lint performs: https://github.com/ansible-community/ansible-lint/blob/main/docs/rules/index.rst
- **Configuring Ansible-lint:** How to tailor its behavior: https://docs.ansible.com/ansible-lint/

Making Lint Part of Your Workflow

- **Integrate with Your Editor:** Many code editors have plugins for real-time linting.
- **Version Control Hooks:** Run Ansible-lint to automatically check code before anyone commits changes.

- **Regular Checkups:** Even for legacy playbooks, a lint run can reveal potential issues to address proactively.

Important Caveat!

Ansible-lint is a powerful tool, but it's not a substitute for thoroughly testing your playbooks. Think of it as an extra layer of protection, not a magic bullet for perfect automation.

Hands-On Exercise: Mastering Playbook Composition

It's time to roll up your sleeves and build a real Ansible playbook. Remember, our focus is on understanding the **structure** and **flow** of playbooks, not complex tasks at this stage.

Prerequisites

- **Ansible Control Machine:** Set up with Ansible installed.
- **Target Servers:** At least one machine you can access as root via SSH (a local VM is fine for practice).
- **Basic Inventory:** Just an IP address under a group in your `hosts` file will do.
- **Ansible-lint:** (Recommended)

Scenario: Simple Website Setup

Let's build a playbook to achieve the following:

1. **Install Apache (or Nginx, based on the target OS)**
2. **Copy a Basic Website:** A simple HTML file you provide is placed in the website's directory.
3. **Start and Enable the Web Service:** Ensure the web server is running and starts on boot.

Step 1: Playbook Skeleton

Create a new file named `website.yml`:

```yaml
---
- hosts: webservers        # Target your inventory group
  become: yes              # Most server admin tasks need elevated privileges
```

```
  vars:
    website_root: /var/www/html   # Adjust if needed

  tasks:
      # Our tasks to achieve the scenario goals will go here
```

Step 2: Tackle the Tasks

- **Task 1:** Ansible has modules like `package` and `yum`, depending on your target systems. You'll likely need conditionals (`when: ansible_os_family == 'Debian'`).
- **Task 2:** The copy module is your friend. Make sure the website file exists on your Ansible Control machine first!
- **Task 3:** Look into the `service` module for managing services across operating systems.

Step 3: Error-Checking

1. **Use `ansible-lint`:** Fix any warnings/errors it finds *before* running the playbook!
2. **Test in Stages:** Run with `--check` mode. Add tasks one by one, re-running to verify each step works in isolation.

Troubleshooting is Part of the Game!

Expect to hit some snags – that's how you learn. Here's how to debug effectively:

- **Read the Error Messages:** Ansible tries to be helpful.
- **The Docs are Your Ally:** Search Ansible module documentation for correct usage and examples.

- **Use the debug Module:** Print variable values if things aren't working as expected.

Beyond the Basics

Here are some ways to spice up the exercise and explore more playbook features:

- **Version Pinning:** Introduce a variable for the webserver package version.
- **User Input:** Try using `-e` during `ansible-playbook` to set the desired website file at runtime.
- **Custom Website:** Write a few lines of basic HTML (`index.html`) to use as your sample website content.

Important: Focus on understanding *why* you structure things a certain way, not blindly copying a solution.

Navigating Choices: Conditional Logic in Ansible

Imagine your Ansible playbooks as an adventurer at a crossroads. Conditionals are the maps that let them decide: should I install the sturdy 'Apache' shield or the swift 'Nginx' one? This chapter is about those decision moments.

The Essence of 'When'

At its heart, conditional logic in Ansible tasks boils down to:

```
tasks:
  - name: Install a webserver
    package:
      name: "{{ 'apache2' if ansible_os_family == 'Debian' else 'nginx' }}"
      state: present
    when: ansible_distribution != 'Windows' # We skip on Windows servers
```

Observations:

- **when:** Is the magic word to introduce a condition.
- **Jinja2 Expressions:** You can use variables and facts within the when:. We'll revisit templating later, but for now, know that the {{ }} are for dynamic content.
- **Comparison Operators:** ==, !=, >, <, etc., let you check things like operating systems.

Common Use Cases

1. **OS-Specific Actions:** Just like the example, tailoring installations or configurations.

2. **Environment Differences:** "If this is production, be extra cautious."
3. **Error Handling:** "If the update failed, send a notification."
4. **Fact-Based Decisions:** "If the server has less than 500MB of free memory, skip the backup task."

Beyond Simple Comparisons

Ansible supports more complex logic:

- **and / or:** Combine multiple conditions: `when: ansible_os_family == 'RedHat' and ansible_distribution_version >= '8'`
- **String Testing:** Is a version number 'latest'? Use `version_compare` within Jinja2 expressions.
- **File Existence:** `exists`, `isdir`, `isfile` – great for task dependencies.

Tips & Tricks

- **Test Thoroughly:** Conditionals mean multiple paths your playbook can take. Test each scenario!
- **debug is Your Friend:** Print the results of your conditional expressions to make sure the logic behaves as intended.
- **Start Simple:** Complex conditionals get hard to read fast. Break them into smaller steps if needed.

Additional Resources

- **Jinja2 Built-in Tests:** The official Jinja2 docs list all the nifty things you can check within your conditions: https://jinja.palletsprojects.com/en/3.0.x/templates/#builtin-tests
- **Ansible Facts:** https://docs.ansible.com/ansible/latest/user_guide/playbooks_vars_facts.html#ansible-facts

Crafting Dynamic Scenarios: Advanced Conditionals and Variable Utilization

In the previous chapter, we dipped our toes into conditional logic. Now, let's dive deeper, combining the power of conditionals with variables to make your playbooks incredibly responsive to their environment.

Scenario: Customized Deployment

Imagine you're managing web servers with varying needs:

- **Some Need a Database Installed:** Others connect to an existing one.
- **App Versions Differ:** Production might be on 1.2, while development runs on the latest 1.5.
- **Monitoring Is Optional:** Smaller servers might skip it to save resources.

Making Your Playbook Adapt

1. **Variables as Switches**

```
vars:
  install_database: true
  app_version: "1.2"
  enable_monitoring: false
```

2. **Conditional Tasks**

```
- name: Install MariaDB
  package:
    name: mariadb-server
```

```
      state: present
  when: install_database == true
```

3. **Templating for Even More Flexibility (we'll cover this later!)**

```
- name: Copy application files (version
specific)
  copy:
    src: "app_v{{ app_version }}"
    dest: /var/www/html
```

Key Ideas

- **Predefine Your Choices:** Variables hold the settings that will control your playbook's behavior.
- **Think Like a Flowchart:** Conditionals (when) become the decision points that split your task flow.
- **External Input:** Use `-e` during `ansible-playbook` to override these variables for different environments!

Advanced Techniques

- **Fact-Based Conditions:** "Install monitoring only if there are more than 4 CPU cores (`ansible_processor_vcnt > 4`)".
- **Conditionals on Previous Results:** Ansible lets you check if a prior task succeeded/failed and react accordingly. This is getting into error handling territory.
- **Registering Variables to Use Later:** Capture the output of a task (say, an IP address) into a variable and use it within other conditionals.

Combining with Loops (Teaser!)

Imagine a task to install packages from a list defined in a variable. Conditionals within a loop let you install different sets of packages onto different server groups! This is where Ansible gets truly powerful.

Additional Resources

- **Jinja2 Power:** https://jinja.palletsprojects.com/en/3.0.x/templates/#builtin-tests

Up Next: The Conditional Challenge

We'll take a hands-on exercise scenario and craft a playbook that tackles it, using variables to guide its execution on different systems.

Practical Exercise: Crafting Conditional Masterpieces

Let's solidify your understanding of conditionals by turning a realistic automation challenge into a playbook full of dynamic decisions.

Scenario: Flexible Backup System

Our mission is to design a playbook to handle backups with the following requirements:

1. **Different Backup Destinations:**
   - Production servers back up to a secure offsite storage service.
   - Development servers back up to a local network share.
2. **Optional Database Backups:** Enabled or disabled per server group.
3. **Compression Level:** High compression for development, low for production (faster backups).

Step 1: Setting the Stage

- **Inventory:** You'll need groups like "production" and "development." Consider adding some host-level variables to control whether individual hosts should have their database backed up (`backup_database: true`)
- **Playbook Outline (Example)**

```yaml
- hosts: all
  vars:
    backup_dest: "local_share"  # Default
    compression: 9              # Default
```

```
    tasks:
      - name: Install backup tools
        package: ...   # Some backup tool
        when: ansible_os_family == 'Debian'   # Only if needed

      - name: Set production backup destination
        set_fact:   # We'll cover 'set_fact' for dynamic variables
          backup_dest: "offsite_storage"
        when: group_names == ['production']

      # ... more tasks for doing the actual backup, using variables conditionally ...
```

Step 2: Tackle the Tasks

You'll likely need to research modules that do backups. Here's where the challenge gets focused on conditionals, not the backup solution itself:

- **Backup Destination:** A task that sets a variable (e.g., `set_fact`), which a later backup task uses to determine where to send files.
- **Backing up the Database:** A conditional task that uses a database backup module, controlled by a group or host-level variable.
- **Compression:** Module options will likely be conditional on the `compression` variable.

Step 3: Test, Test, Test!

- **Multiple Environments:** If possible, set up target VMs representing both production and development to see your playbook work its magic.
- **Fact Manipulation:** If you use `set_fact` during the play, use debug to ensure your variables are changing as expected.

Beyond the Basics

- **Error Handling:** What if a backup task fails? Write conditionals to send alerts or trigger cleanup tasks based on failure.
- **Rolling Backups:** For mission-critical systems, only delete old backups *after* a new one is confirmed successful.

Tips

- **Deliberate Mistakes:** Introduce errors into your playbook's logic to test your understanding of how Ansible evaluates conditionals.
- **Draw it Out:** If the conditional logic gets complex, a simple flowchart can help you visualize the desired playbook flow.

Embracing Repetition: Looping Constructs, Part 1

Imagine you need to install a list of packages, or create multiple similar users. Doing this manually in a playbook would be tedious and prone to errors. Loops are Ansible's way of saying, "Let's do this thing, but repeatedly!"

The Power of Iteration

Loops let you automate tasks that follow a pattern. Key benefits:

- **Less Typing:** Define the action once, apply it to many items.
- **Reduced Errors:** Fewer places for typos to cause mayhem.
- **Scalability:** Your playbook handles 5 servers or 500 with the same ease.
- **Dynamic with Variables:** Loop over lists of things stored in variables, making your playbooks incredibly flexible.

The Basic 'Loop'

Let's start with the simplest, most common loop usage:

```
tasks:
  - name: Install a list of packages
    package:
      name: "{{ item }}"
      state: present
    with_items:
      - httpd
      - php
      - mariadb
```

Breakdown

- `with_items:` The magic keyword that introduces a basic loop.
- `{{ item }}`: A placeholder variable. On each loop iteration, it will hold the next value from the list (first 'httpd', then 'php', and so on).
- **Indentation is King:** Tasks within the loop are indented to show they're part of the repeated structure.

Looping Beyond Packages

Ansible loops are incredibly versatile. Here's a taste:

- **Creating Users:** `user: name: "{{ item }}" state: present` with a list of usernames.
- **Configuring Files:** Use the `template` module and loop over lines to insert into a configuration file.
- **Calling Other Modules:** Many Ansible modules let you loop over internal actions for powerful effects.

Pro Tip: Don't Overthink It

In the beginning, think of loops as a "for each thing in this list, do this task" mechanism.

Additional Resources

- **Ansible Loops Doc:** Details all the ways you can customize loops: https://docs.ansible.com/ansible/latest/user_guide/playbooks_loops.html

Up Next - Iterative Intelligence: In Part 2, we'll explore how to get information from previous loop iterations, how to filter what you loop over, and more loop superpowers.

Diving Deeper into Iterations: Looping Constructs, Part 2

In the previous chapter, we learned the basics of looping over lists. Now, let's unlock some techniques that will transform your playbooks from repetitive to downright ingenious.

Looping with Complex Data

Often you won't have simple lists of packages. Let's say you have a variable in your inventory like this:

```
app_servers:
  - hostname: server1.example.com
    port: 80
  - hostname: server2.example.com
    port: 8080
```

And you want to open firewall ports on each:

```
tasks:
  - name: Open firewall ports for the app
    firewalld:
      port: "{{ item.port }}/tcp"
      permanent: true
      state: enabled
```

```
    with_dict: "{{ app_servers }}"
```

- **`with_dict`:** Tells Ansible to loop over a dictionary (key-value pairs).
- **`item.port`:** Within the loop, `item` becomes a temporary variable holding each server's details.

Accessing Old Values: 'loop.index0'

Imagine installing packages, but *skipping* the first one. This is where Ansible's loop variables come in:

```
- name: Install packages (skip the first)
  package:
    name: "{{ packages }}"
    state: present
  with_items: "{{ packages }}"
  when: loop.index0 > 0   # Zero-based index
```

Registers to the Rescue

What if you need a task's *output* within the loop? Use `register` (like you may have for variable capture before):

```
- name: Get installed package versions
  package_facts:
  register: installed_pkgs
```

```
- name: Print package versions
  debug:
    msg: "{{ item.0 }} is at version {{ item.1.version }}"
  with_together:
    - "{{ installed_pkgs.ansible_facts.packages }}"
    - "{{ installed_pkgs.ansible_facts.packages.keys() }}"
```

- **with_together:** Lets you loop over multiple lists at once. Tricky to grasp initially, but powerful!

Filtering While Looping

Use when within a loop to act only on certain items:

```
- name: Delete large log files
  file:
    path: "/var/log/{{ item }}"
    state: absent
  with_fileglob:
    - "/var/log/*.log"
  when: item.size > 1000000  # Only if over 1MB
```

Additional Resources

- **Jinja2 in Loops:** If your data is complex, learning a bit more Jinja2 will let you reshape how you loop over it: https://docs.ansible.com/ansible/latest/user_guide/playbooks_loops.html#templating-with-jinja2-in-loops
- **Nested Loops:** https://docs.ansible.com/ansible/latest/user_guide/playbooks_loops.html#nested-loops

Up Next: The Iteration Challenge

It's time for a hands-on exercise where you must combine loops, conditionals, and perhaps even variable registration to achieve a multi-step automation task.

Hands-On Challenge: Iterative Brilliance with Ansible Loops

It's time to test your Ansible loop mastery with a scenario that demands flexibility and a touch of cleverness.

Scenario: Patch Management

Your task is to write a playbook with these capabilities:

1. **Applies Available Updates:** Uses your system's package management module (`yum` or `apt` based on OS) to install security updates.
2. **Pre-Update Backups:** For each server, creates a simple backup of a specified configuration directory before updating.
3. **Selective Reboots:** Only reboots the server if the update module reports that a reboot is required.

Requirements

- **Inventory:** Groups for different OS families (e.g., "redhat_servers", "debian_servers").
- **Variables:** A variable like `config_backup_dir: "/etc/myapp"` to set what gets backed up.
- **Conditionals:** For OS-specific tasks and reboot logic.
- **Loops:** For iterating over your servers, potentially nested loops.
- **Fact Gathering:** You might need to gather facts about installed packages.

Step-by-Step Approach

1. **The Update Core:** A task using a package module like `apt`, with a loop over your servers. Consider registering the result to determine if updates were even applied.
2. **Back It Up:** A task using the `synchronize` module (or similar) to copy the `config_backup_dir` to a destination on the Ansible control machine, perhaps into a server-specific folder. This likely runs *before* the update task.
3. **Reboot If Needed:** A final task using the `reboot` module or a command via `shell`, with a `when:` conditional that checks if the registered update result indicates a reboot requirement *(this part is OS-dependent!)*

Tips

- **Test Incrementally:** Build the playbook task by task, testing on sample servers.
- **Fake the Updates:** Use `-C` with `ansible-playbook` for a dry run initially to avoid disruptive updates while developing.
- **Simplify at First:** Maybe skip the backup part until you have the update and reboot logic.

Advanced Options

- **Error Handling:** What if the backup fails? Should you even attempt updates then?
- **Notifications:** Send a success/failure report via Slack or email integration (this gets into more Ansible features).
- **Update Filtering:** Perhaps only update packages matching a certain pattern ("kernel" updates might be higher risk).

Don't Get Stuck

Focus on understanding *why* you're doing each step more than perfect syntax initially. Ansible docs and searching online for similar examples are your allies!

Section 6: Harnessing the Power of Ansible Modules

Unveiling the Arsenal: Exploring Ansible Modules, Part 1

Think of Ansible modules as your toolbox, each tool ready to tackle a specific infrastructure task. In this chapter, we'll start unwrapping that toolbox, learning how to find the right module for the job and the basics of how to use them.

What Exactly *Are* Modules?

- **Self-Contained Automation Units:** Each module knows how to manage one aspect of a system – installing packages, configuring files, managing users, etc.
- **Not Just Scripts:** They are often written in Python and provide a clean way to interact with your systems, hiding some of the underlying complexity.
- **Batteries Included:** Ansible ships with hundreds of built-in modules to cover the most common infrastructure tasks.

Module Hunting 101

1. **The Ansible Docs Are Your Guide:** The module index is the best place to start: https://docs.ansible.com/ansible/latest/modules/modules_by_category.html

2. **Search by Task, Not Technology:** Do you need to "manage a package" or "copy a file"? Search with those terms rather than obsessing over specific OS commands initially.
3. **Examples are Golden:** Module documentation pages almost always include clear examples of how they're used in playbooks.

Anatomy of a Module Task

Let's break down a common use of the `file` module:

```
- name: Ensure configuration directory exists
  file:
    path: /etc/my_app/conf
    state: directory
    mode: '0750'
```

- `file:` The module name. This is our tool!
- `path`, `state`, `mode`: These are module *parameters* or *options*. They control the module's behavior (what file/directory, its desired state, permissions, etc.).

Key Module Concepts

- **Idempotence:** Most modules strive to only make changes if needed. Run this task twice, and the second time nothing should actually happen since the directory already exists.
- **State:** Modules often work with the idea of a desired state ("this file should exist", "this service should be running").
- **Returns:** Modules provide feedback in the form of Ansible task results. This lets you use those results with conditionals or variable registration.

Popular Module Categories

- **Package Management:** apt, yum, `pip`, etc.

- **File Manipulation:** `copy`, `file`, `synchronize`
- **Service Control:** `service`, `systemd`
- **Cloud Interaction:** A vast array of modules for various cloud providers exist!
- **And Many More:** Networking, templating, database interaction...

Additional Resources

- **Beyond the Built-ins:** Ansible Galaxy is the hub for community-created roles and modules: https://galaxy.ansible.com/

Expanding Your Toolkit: Exploring Ansible Modules, Part 2

In the previous chapter, we got our feet wet exploring Ansible's built-in modules. Now, it's time to expand our horizons and tackle slightly more complex tasks.

Scenario: Basic Server Setup

Let's imagine you often provision new Linux servers. Here's a playbook outline for some initial setup steps:

```yaml
---
- hosts: new_servers

  tasks:
    - name: Install common utilities
      apt:   # Assuming Debian-based
        name: "{{ packages }}"
        state: present
      with_items:
        - net-tools
        - vim
        - htop

    - name: Create a deployment user
      user:
        name: deploy_user
        state: present
        groups: sudo  # Might be 'wheel' depending on your OS
        append: yes

    - name: Ensure web content directory exists
      file:
```

```
          path: /var/www
          state: directory
          owner: deploy_user
          group: deploy_user
```

Observations

- **Multiple Modules:** We're combining `apt`, `user`, and `file` to accomplish our larger goal.
- **Variables in Play:** Assume a `packages` variable is defined in our inventory or elsewhere.
- **State-Based Thinking:** We're not scripting steps, but telling Ansible what we *want* the end result to be.

Beyond the Basics

1. **Module-Specific Gotchas:** Read the docs carefully. Some modules have requirements (like certain libraries needing to be pre-installed on your target machines).
2. **Controlling Change:** `notify` and `handlers` (which we'll cover later) let you trigger other tasks *only if* a module makes a change. This is great for things like service restarts.
3. **Complex Parameters:** Some modules take lists or dictionaries as input. Learn a bit of YAML syntax to use these effectively.

Pro Tips

- **Test in Stages:** Break your playbook into smaller pieces and test them individually as you add complexity.
- **Don't Reinvent the Wheel:** Before writing a bunch of tasks yourself, search Ansible Galaxy https://galaxy.ansible.com/. There might be a pre-made "role" that does most of what you need!

Illuminating Possibilities: Introduction to Ansible Plugins

You've mastered the core modules that come with Ansible, but what if you need to do something a bit... unusual? That's where plugins come in. Think of them as modular extensions that enhance the very heart of Ansible.

Types of Ansible Plugins

Plugins aren't just about new modules. They add power in several ways:

- **Modules, the Usual Suspects:** Most plugins you'll encounter *do* provide new modules, extending support for specific technologies or cloud providers.
- **Lookup Plugins:** These fetch data from external sources. Imagine a plugin that queries your hardware asset database and injects that as Ansible variables.
- **Connection Plugins:** Control how Ansible communicates with your machines. Need a way to manage network devices instead of Linux servers? There's likely a plugin for that.
- **Callback Plugins:** Modify how Ansible reports status, lets you send notifications to Slack, log to a custom system, etc.
- **And More!** Ansible's plugin architecture is flexible.

Why Plugins Matter

1. **Filling in the Gaps:** Ansible can't have built-in modules for *everything*. Plugins let it integrate with the specific tools *you* use.
2. **Community Power:** You don't have to write every bit of automation yourself. Ansible Galaxy is a hub for community-made plugins.

3. **Advanced Customization:** If your company has very unique processes, you can even write your own plugins.

Plugins in the Wild

- **Cloud Providers:** Major players like AWS, Azure, and Google Cloud all have collections of Ansible plugins for managing their various services.
- **Network Devices:** Plugins exist to manage routers, switches, and firewalls from many vendors directly with Ansible.
- **Data Lookups:** Plugins that pull info from systems like HashiCorp Vault (for secrets) or ServiceNow (asset tracking).

Important: Plugins Aren't Always the Answer

Sometimes, a simple module like 'shell' (to run a command) or a template is the more straightforward way to do something non-standard. Plugins add a bit of complexity.

Finding Plugins

- **Ansible Galaxy:** The primary hub for community plugins: https://galaxy.ansible.com/
- **Vendor Documentation:** Cloud providers or hardware vendors often maintain their own collections of Ansible plugins.

Coding Expedition: Exploring Ansible Modules in Action

It's time to embark on an automation adventure! Get ready to translate module knowledge into tangible results with hands-on scenarios that test your Ansible skills.

Prerequisites

- **Ansible Control Machine:** Your command center, all set up.
- **Target Systems:** A few VMs or, ideally, machines on your network to orchestrate. Having a mix of operating systems (e.g., Ubuntu and CentOS) is a bonus.
- **Adventurer's Spirit:** Focus on problem-solving and experimentation!

Scenario 1: Health Checkup

Goal: Craft a playbook that gathers essential health information about your target servers.

- **Uptime:**
    - The `command` or `shell` module are your allies for executing 'uptime'. Remember to register the output for further use.
    - Can you extract the relevant load average numbers from the output? String manipulation within Ansible might come in handy.
- **Disk Space:**
    - Start with the `df` command.
    - For advanced filtering (e.g., only show filesystems above 80% usage), the `stat` module might offer more refined control.

- **Service Status:**
    - The `service` module is your go-to. Ensure you have a clearly defined list of critical services to monitor based on your infrastructure.

Scenario 2: Streamlining User Setup

Goal: Build a playbook to automate the tedious onboarding steps for new developer machines.

- **Account Creation:**
    - Dive into the `user` module's capabilities.
    - Pay attention to `groups`, managing their default shell (`shell`), and how you'd approach password handling (`password_hash`). Is there a way to fetch secure passwords from an external vault using a plugin?
- **Standard Packages:**
    - Leverage `apt`, `yum`, or your OS-specific package module.
    - Define your core package list as a variable for easy modification.
- **SSH Key:**
    - The `authorized_key` module streamlines adding developer SSH keys.
    - Think about *where* these keys are stored and how to securely incorporate them into your playbook.

Pro Tips

- **Iterate and Test:** Build playbooks step-by-step, rigorously testing each task.
- **OS-Aware:** Module behavior changes across operating systems. Refer to documentation for OS-specific quirks.

- **The Power of Debug:** Printing intermediate results with the debug module is your secret weapon to understand the flow of data within your playbooks.

Expand Your Horizons

- **Reporting:** Could you integrate a plugin to have your playbook send a summary notification (Slack, email, etc.)?
- **Idempotence FTW:** Re-run your playbooks. Do they make unnecessary changes? How could you ensure they only act when truly required?
- **Templating:** For complex configurations, consider a templating exercise (we'll cover this later!) to generate config files dynamically.

The True Treasure

This chapter's focus isn't merely about syntax, but developing these crucial skills:

1. **Module Discovery:** Solidifying your ability to hunt down the perfect module for the task.
2. **Doc Comprehension:** Learning to extract vital information from module documentation.
3. **Ansible in Action:** Experiencing the Ansible workflow, from idempotence to how variables interact with modules in real-world scenarios.

Section 7:
Orchestrating with Finesse: Handlers, Roles, and Collections

Mastering the Art of Responsiveness: An Insight into Handlers

In the grand symphony of Ansible automation, handlers are like the subtle percussionists. They add nuanced responses to the changes your playbooks orchestrate. Handlers are special tasks designed to execute only when triggered, ensuring your infrastructure remains in its desired state.

Understanding the Need for Handlers

Picture this scenario: You're updating a web server's configuration file as part of a larger Ansible playbook. While the file is updated, what if you also need to restart the web service to apply changes? Without handlers, you might chain additional tasks within your playbook. This can make things less modular and less efficient.

Handlers come to the rescue! They let you define actions to be taken *if and only if* other tasks within your playbook notify them of changes. This leads to cleaner, more streamlined playbooks.

Anatomy of a Handler

Let's dissect the structure of a handler:

```
handlers:
  - name: restart web service
    service:
      name: httpd
      state: restarted
    listen: "update web config"
```

- **name:** A descriptive identifier for your handler.
- **task(s):** Actions to be executed, like using the 'service' module to restart a service. These tasks are identical to regular playbook tasks.
- **listen:** A unique string or list of strings. Your handler 'listens' for notifications with these names.

Triggering Change: The 'notify' Directive

Tasks within your playbook trigger handlers using the `notify` directive:

```
- name: Update web server configuration
  copy:
    src: webconfig.conf
    dest: /etc/webserver/
  notify: restart web service
```

When the 'Update web server configuration' task modifies the configuration file, it sends a notification with the name 'restart web service'. Any handler listening for that exact notification string will now be executed.

Handler Execution and Idempotency

- **When do they run?** Handlers are executed only once at the *end* of a playbook run, even if notified multiple times. This streamlines your workflow.
- **Idempotency:** Handlers, like regular tasks, aim to be idempotent. This means running them repeatedly should

lead to the same desired system state, minimizing unnecessary actions.

Handler Strategies

1. **Restarting Services:** A classic use case, ensuring that services reflect configuration updates.
2. **Cleanup Tasks:** Removing temporary files or configurations no longer needed.
3. **Logging & Reporting:** Sending notifications or updating logs based on changes.
4. **Conditional Execution:** Handlers can use conditions like regular tasks, adding further control over their behavior.

Best Practices

- **Descriptive Names:** Clear names for both handlers and the `notify` values make your playbooks easier to understand.
- **Strategic Placement:** Place handlers logically in your playbook structure for maintainability.
- **Avoid Over-Reliance:** Handlers are powerful, but sometimes simple sequential tasks within a playbook are better. Find the right balance.

Hands-On Exercise

- Create a playbook to install a package and define a handler to start the relevant service if the package installation results in a change.

Additional Resources

- **Ansible Documentation - Handlers:** https://docs.ansible.com/ansible/latest/user_guide/playbooks_handlers.html

- **Blog on Ansible Handlers with Examples:** https://docs.ansible.com/ansible/latest/playbook_guide/playbooks_handlers.html

Crafting Reusable Solutions: Understanding Ansible Roles, Part 1

As your IT infrastructure grows and your Ansible playbooks become more sophisticated, you might find yourself repeating similar sets of tasks—configuring web servers, installing databases, or setting up monitoring tools. Ansible Roles introduce a powerful solution to streamline automation and promote code reuse across your playbooks and your team.

The Essence of Ansible Roles

Imagine Ansible Roles as modular building blocks. A role encapsulates a well-defined set of tasks, variables, configuration files, templates, and other resources necessary to achieve a specific infrastructure state. Think of a role as a blueprint for configuring a particular service or component of your system.

Why Use Ansible Roles?

1. **Reusability:** Write a role once and use it in multiple playbooks. This significantly reduces code duplication, saving you time and effort.
2. **Organization:** Roles impose a clear structure, making your automation code more organized, maintainable, and easier to understand.
3. **Shareability:** Ansible Galaxy (https://galaxy.ansible.com/) is a hub for sharing roles. You can tap into a vast collection of community-created roles and contribute your own, boosting collaboration and efficiency.

Anatomy of an Ansible Role

Ansible roles adhere to a specific directory structure for consistency. Here's a breakdown of the most common directories:

- **tasks:** Contains the core playbooks tasks that will be executed by the role. The primary file here is usually `main.yml`.
- **handlers:** Contains handler definitions (covered in the previous chapter) specific to this role.
- **defaults:** Houses default variables for the role, often found in `main.yml`. These variables have lower precedence, allowing easy customization.
- **vars:** Holds variables with higher precedence, often in `main.yml`, for more control when necessary.
- **files:** Stores static files that your tasks might need, like configuration files or scripts.
- **templates:** Holds Jinja2 templates for generating dynamic configuration files (more on this in later chapters).
- **meta:** Contains metadata about the role (author, dependencies, etc.), usually in `main.yml`.

Creating Your First Role

The quickest way to get started is using the `ansible-galaxy` tool:

1. **Initialization:** `ansible-galaxy init my_webserver_role` (replace 'my_webserver_role' with your role name)
2. **Explore:** Examine the generated directory structure.
3. **Populate:** Place your tasks, handlers, files, and templates within the appropriate directories.

Including Roles in a Playbook

```
- hosts: webservers
  roles:
```

```
      - my_webserver_role
```

Part 2 and Beyond

In 'Part 2' of this exploration, we'll delve into advanced role usage like:

- Parameterizing roles for flexibility
- Role dependencies
- Best practices for crafting maintainable roles

Hands-On Exercise

- Use `ansible-galaxy init` to create a role named 'basic_security'.
- Populate it with tasks to enforce basic security settings (e.g., updating packages, setting firewall rules).
- Write a playbook that includes and applies the 'basic_security' role.

Additional Resources

- **Ansible Documentation - Roles:**
  https://docs.ansible.com/ansible/latest/user_guide/playbooks_reuse_roles.html

Scaling Your Infrastructure: Understanding Ansible Roles, Part 2

In the previous chapter, we laid the foundation of Ansible Roles. Now let's explore how roles empower you to manage growing complexity as your infrastructure expands and your automation requirements evolve.

Parameterizing Your Roles

Think of role parameters as the dials and knobs allowing you to customize a role's behavior. By defining default variables within your role's `defaults/main.yml` file and then overriding them during playbook execution, you create highly adaptable solutions.

Example: Web Server Role Parameterization

```yaml
# defaults/main.yml (within your web server role)
http_port: 80
document_root: /var/www/html
```

```yaml
# Your Playbook
- hosts: webservers
  roles:
    - role: my_webserver_role
      http_port: 8080  # Overrides the default
```

Key Points on Parameterization

- **Flexibility:** Adapt roles to different environments or use cases.

- **Maintainability:** Make changes from the playbook level, keeping your core role logic intact.

Role Dependencies

Complex systems involve interconnected components. Role dependencies enable you to express relationships between roles. One role might require that another role is executed beforehand.

Example: Database Dependency

```
- hosts: appservers
  roles:
    - { role: database_setup, when: install_database == 'yes' }
    - my_application_role
```

Notes on Dependencies

- **Sequencing:** Ensure proper setup orders (e.g., the database needs to exist before the application that uses it).
- **Conditionals:** Control dependency execution based on variables for fine-grained control.

Structuring Projects for Scale

As your project grows, consider these organizational strategies:

1. **Role per Service/Component:** Maintain focus and increase reusability (web server role, monitoring role, etc.).
2. **Repositories:** Use a version control system like Git for your roles, promoting collaboration, history, and rollbacks if needed.
3. **Ansible Galaxy:** Share roles internally using a private Galaxy server or publicly on the community Galaxy hub (https://galaxy.ansible.com/).

Advanced Tips

- **'include_role' vs. 'import_role':** These similar tasks have subtle differences in when variables and tasks are loaded. Explore their nuances for precise control.
- **Role Testing:** Frameworks like Molecule (https://molecule.readthedocs.io/) help you write tests for your roles, ensuring quality.

Hands-On Challenge

- Refactor your 'basic_security' role from the previous exercise to:
    - Accept parameters for which firewall ports to open.
    - Include a role to install essential security tools like 'fail2ban' as a dependency.

Additional Resources

- **Ansible Documentation - Role Dependencies:** https://docs.ansible.com/ansible/latest/user_guide/playbooks_reuse_roles.html#role-dependencies
- **Ansible Galaxy Best Practices:** https://docs.ansible.com/ansible/latest/user_guide/playbooks_best_practices.html#ansible-galaxy-best-practices

Embracing Innovation: Unveiling Ansible Collections

Ansible Collections represent the next evolution in packaging and distributing Ansible content. Think of them as 'power-up packs' that neatly bundle roles, modules, plugins, and documentation for a specific technology or domain. Collections streamline automation development and promote community collaboration like never before.

Why Collections Matter

- **Organization:** Collections introduce greater modularity. Rather than monolithic Ansible projects, you can work with focused, well-defined units of automation logic.
- **Sharing and Reuse:** Ansible Galaxy (https://galaxy.ansible.com/) becomes your go-to resource for certified and community Collections. Find ready-to-use automation components and effortlessly share yours.
- **Decoupling:** Collections can be developed and released independently of core Ansible releases, promoting rapid innovation and targeted solutions.

Anatomy of a Collection

A collection has a standardized directory structure (you can use `ansible-galaxy collection init` to generate one):

- **README.md:** Informative overview of the collection.
- **docs/:** Documentation for the included content in the collection.
- **galaxy.yml:** Metadata (author, version, dependencies on other collections).
- **playbooks/:** Holds sample playbooks or usage examples.

- **roles/:** Where your Ansible Roles reside, as we've explored.
- **plugins/:** Location for custom Ansible plugins (we'll cover plugins later).
- **tests/:** Directory for tests to ensure the collection's quality.

Using Collections

1. **Installation:** `ansible-galaxy collection install namespace.collection_name` (e.g., `ansible-galaxy collection install community.general`)
2. **Referencing Content:** Use a fully qualified name:

```yaml
- hosts: firewalls
  collections:
    - fortinet.fortios
  tasks:
    - name: Configure firewall policy
      fortios_firewall_policy:
        # Module parameters here
```

Creating Your Own Collection

1. **Initialization:** `ansible-galaxy collection init my_networking_tools`
2. **Populate:** Add your roles, modules, plugins, etc. to the appropriate directories.
3. **Build and Publish:** Use the `ansible-galaxy collection build` command to create a distributable tarball and then share it on Ansible Galaxy or your private repositories!

Tips for Success

- **Start with Community Collections:** Explore Ansible Galaxy to get a feel for great collections and their structure.

- **Namespace Wisely:** Use namespaces (like `yourcompany.collection_name`) to prevent naming conflicts.
- **Documentation Matters:** Invest time in writing clear documentation within your collection's 'docs/' directory.

Hands-On Challenge

1. Search Ansible Galaxy for a collection relevant to a technology you use (e.g., networking, cloud providers, etc.).
2. Install the collection.
3. Write a small playbook using a few modules or roles from the collection.

Additional Resources

- **Ansible Documentation - Collections:** https://docs.ansible.com/ansible/latest/collections_guide/index.html
- **Ansible Galaxy:** https://galaxy.ansible.com/

Practical Challenge: Harnessing the Power of Handlers, Roles, and Collections

It's time to test your mettle and solidify your understanding of Ansible's core components. In this comprehensive challenge, you'll create a scenario that brings together the elegant interplay between handlers, roles, and collections.

The Scenario: WordPress Deployment with Monitoring

Objectives

1. Install and configure a WordPress instance on a set of web servers.
2. Create a mechanism to restart the web service (Apache/Nginx) whenever the WordPress configuration changes.
3. Utilize a collection to install and configure a monitoring agent for collecting metrics and checking service health.

Building the Solution

1. Project Setup

- Create a new directory for your project.
- Inside, create an Ansible playbook (e.g., `wordpress_deployment.yml`).

2. The Web Server Role

- Create a role named `wordpress`.
- **Tasks:**

- Install necessary packages (Apache/Nginx, PHP, MySQL client, etc.).
- Download and extract WordPress.
- Configure WordPress (`wp-config.php`).
- Set up virtual host or server block.
- **Handler:**
  - Name: Restart web service
  - Use the appropriate service module (`service` or equivalent).
  - Listen for notifications from WordPress configuration tasks.

3. Monitoring Role

- Search Ansible Galaxy for a suitable monitoring collection (e.g., `community.general`, `prometheus`, or vendor-specific ones).
- Install the selected collection (`ansible-galaxy collection install ...`).
- Create a `monitoring` role.
- **Tasks:**
  - Use the collection's modules to install and configure the monitoring agent.
  - Configure the agent to monitor the web service and core system metrics.

4. The Playbook

```
- hosts: webservers
  roles:
    - wordpress
    - monitoring
```

Execution and Workflow

1. Run your playbook.

2. Make intentional modifications to the WordPress configuration files.
3. Observe the handler restarting the web service.
4. Verify monitoring functionality from the collection you used.

Tips

- **Variables:** Use variables to parameterize database names, WordPress paths, monitoring thresholds, etc.
- **Idempotency:** Ensure tasks can be safely rerun, updating resources only when actually changed.
- **Error Handling:** Consider using blocks with error recovery for a robust solution.

Beyond the Basics

- **Templating:** Use Jinja2 templating (covered later) for dynamic configuration of WordPress settings and the monitoring agent.
- **Security:** Include a role from a security collection or create one to harden your WordPress setup.
- **Continuous Delivery:** Extend this into a pipeline where code changes trigger an automated Ansible deployment process (a more advanced topic for exploration).

Additional Resources

- **Ansible Documentation - Best practices:** https://docs.ansible.com/ansible/latest/user_guide/playbooks_best_practices.html
- **Community Collections on Ansible Galaxy:** https://galaxy.ansible.com/

Level Up!

Modify the challenge to install a database server using a role and make WordPress installation dependent on it.

Unveiling the Secrets of Templating

Thus far, we've primarily used static configuration files and task definitions. Imagine the power of dynamically generating configurations, injecting variables, and adapting content based on conditions. Templating with Ansible unlocks this potential, empowering you to craft truly adaptable solutions.

Jinja2: The Templating Engine

Ansible leverages the Jinja2 templating engine. Jinja2 brings a robust programming-like language directly into your Ansible playbooks and configuration files.

Key Concepts

1. **Variables:** Wrapped in double curly braces `{{ }}`.
   Example: `DocumentRoot: {{ web_root_path }}`
2. **Control Structures:** For logic and iterations.
   Example:

   ```
   {% for user in users %}
     user: {{ user.name }}
   {% endfor %}
   ```

3. **Filters:** Modify or transform data.
   Example: `{{ package_name | upper }}` (converts the package name to uppercase)

Where to Use Templating

- **Configuration Files:** Create files for web servers, applications, databases, etc., with settings injected at runtime.
- **Task Definitions:** Make task parameters dynamic. For example, a file path from a variable.
- **Playbook Names (limited):** Introduce some dynamism into playbook naming.

The 'template' Module

The `template` module is your primary tool for Ansible templating:

```
- name: Deploy Nginx configuration
  template:
    src: nginx.conf.j2  # Jinja2 template
    dest: /etc/nginx/nginx.conf
```

Tips and Tricks

- **Whitespace Control:** Jinja2 has features to prevent extra lines or unwanted spaces in your output. Explore `trim_blocks` and `lstrip_blocks`.
- **Complex Data Structures:** Create lists and dictionaries within your Ansible variables and loop over them or access elements within templates.
- **Testing:** Temporarily render your templates with variables for quick previews and troubleshooting.

Hands-On Exercise

1. Create a simple Jinja2 template (`server.conf.j2`) for a configuration file.
2. Insert variables for server name, port, and document root.

3. Write a playbook with the `template` module and sample variables to generate the configuration file.

Advanced Templating

- **Lookups:** Fetch data from external sources (CSV, APIs, etc.) with lookup plugins.
- **Custom Filters:** Extend Jinja2 by creating your own filters for specialized transformations.
- **Macros:** Think of them as reusable functions within your templates.

Additional Resources

- **Ansible Documentation - Templating**
  https://docs.ansible.com/ansible/latest/user_guide/playbooks_templating.html
- **Jinja2 Documentation:**
  https://jinja.palletsprojects.com/en/2.11.x/

Crafting Dynamic Configurations with Jinja2 Templates: Hands-On Demo, Part 1

Prerequisites

- Basic Ansible playbook understanding.
- A text editor or IDE to modify files.
- A test environment (local machine, virtual machine, or a small cloud instance).

Scenario: Customizing Your Web Server Configuration

Our goal will be to create a dynamic template for an Nginx or Apache virtual host configuration file. We'll focus on the following:

1. **Injecting Dynamic Variables:** Server name, document root, and listening port.
2. **Conditional Logic:** Including optional configuration blocks based on variables.

Setting the Stage

1. **Variables:**

```
server_domain: www.example.com
web_root: /var/www/html
listen_port: 80
enable_ssl: false  # For conditional logic later
```

2. **Template Structure (nginx.conf.j2):**

```
server {
    listen {{ listen_port }};
    server_name {{ server_domain }};
    root {{ web_root }};

    # ... other common directives ...
}
```

The Playbook

```
- hosts: webservers
  tasks:
    - name: Generate and deploy web server configuration
      template:
        src: nginx.conf.j2
        dest: /etc/nginx/sites-available/mysite.conf
      # ... (optional) notify a handler to reload Nginx ...
```

Part 1 Focus: Variables and Conditionals

1. **Run and Observe:** Execute your playbook. Examine the generated configuration in `/etc/nginx/sites-available/mysite.conf`.
2. **Conditional Configuration:** Expand your template with an SSL block:

```
{% if enable_ssl == true %}
# SSL Configuration
listen 443 ssl;
ssl_certificate /path/to/cert.pem;
ssl_certificate_key /path/to/cert.key;
```

```
# ... other SSL directives ...
{% endif %}
```

3. **Rerun and Adapt:** Modify the `enable_ssl` variable and rerun the playbook. Observe how the generated configuration changes.

Key Takeaways

- **The Power of Variables:** Effortlessly modify behavior across your infrastructure.
- **Conditional Logic:** Create configurations tailored to specific environments or requirements.

Hands-On Challenge

- Expand the template to include customizable logging directives based on a 'logging_level' variable (e.g., 'debug', 'info', 'error').

Additional Resources

- **Jinja2 Designer Documentation** (great for testing!): https://jinja.palletsprojects.com/en/2.11.x/templates/

Part 2

In the next chapter, we'll delve into Jinja2 loops for managing lists of items, lookups to pull external data, and advanced templating techniques further customizing your infrastructure.

Crafting Dynamic Configurations with Jinja2 Templates: Hands-On Demo, Part 2

Expanding Our Scenario

Let's imagine managing multiple websites on a single server, each with potentially different requirements. We'll enhance our templating to handle this.

1. Introducing Lists and Loops

Modify your playbook variables:

```
websites:
  - name: www.example.com
    root: /var/www/example_com
    enable_php: true
  - name: myblog.net
    root: /var/www/myblog
```

Update your template (nginx.conf.j2):

```
{% for site in websites %}
server {
    listen 80;
    server_name {{ site.name }};
    root {{ site.root }};

    {% if site.enable_php == true %}
    # PHP Configuration ...
```

```
    {% endif %}
}
{% endfor %}
```

2. Lookups to Fetch External Data

Use Ansible's lookup plugins to pull information from sources like files, databases, or APIs:

```
# Assuming a CSV file 'ssl_certs.csv' exists
{% for site in websites %}
# ... (like before) ...

    {% if site.enable_ssl == true %}
    ssl_certificate {{ lookup('file', 'ssl_certs.csv', search_string=site.name + ',cert_path') }};
    ssl_certificate_key {{ lookup('file', 'ssl_certs.csv', search_string=site.name + ',key_path') }};
    {% endif %}
{% endfor %}
```

Key Takeaways

- **Iteration Power:** Handle multiple similar resources with a single template.
- **External Data:** Integrate information from various sources for streamlined configuration.

Hands-On Challenge

- Research Ansible's 'dict' lookup plugin (https://docs.ansible.com/ansible/latest/collections/ansible/b

uiltin/dict_lookup.html). Use it to store PHP configuration based on version requirements.

Advanced Templating Techniques

- **Macros:** Imagine reusable blocks of Jinja2 code, like functions, making your templates more modular.
- **Custom Filters:** Extend Jinja2 by creating functions to manipulate data in specialized ways relevant to your infrastructure.
- **Template Inheritance:** Create base templates and extend them, promoting consistency and reducing repetition.

Tips

- **Test incrementally:** As complexity grows, test with smaller data sets.
- **Use Jinja2 Designer:** Experiment and visualize your templates before deployment.
- **Explore Examples:** Seek inspiration from online examples and community templates.

Additional Resources

- **Ansible Documentation - Lookup Plugins:** https://docs.ansible.com/ansible/latest/plugins/lookup.html
- **Jinja2 documentation on Macros and Inheritance:** https://jinja.palletsprojects.com/en/2.11.x/

Conclusion

Congratulations! You've journeyed from Ansible novice to a confident automation practitioner. Throughout this book, you have:

- **Grasped the Fundamentals:** You understand Ansible's core concepts, configuration, and YAML, the language of infrastructure as code.
- **Mapped Your Territory:** Inventories have no secrets, allowing you to precisely target your managed systems.
- **Harnessed Variables:** Your playbooks are dynamic, adapting effortlessly to different environments and scenarios.
- **Mastered Orchestration:** Playbooks, conditionals, loops – these are the tools to conduct your automation symphony.
- **Embraced Modules:** Ansible's vast arsenal lets you manage countless technologies with ease.
- **Scaled with Finesse:** Handlers, roles, and collections bring modularity and efficiency to your growing infrastructure.
- **Conquered Configuration:** Templating with Jinja2 puts an end to tedious, error-prone manual configuration.

The Adventure Continues

Your Ansible journey doesn't end here. Automation is a continuous process of refinement and exploration. Here's how you can keep the momentum going:

- **Real-World Applications:** Take the scenarios from this book and apply them to your own projects. Start small and expand your scope.
- **Community Power:** Engage with the vibrant Ansible community on forums, meetups, and AnsibleFest. Share your knowledge and learn from others.

- **Explore the Edge:** Delve into more advanced topics like: * Continuous Integration/Deployment (CI/CD) Pipelines with Ansible * Ansible Tower/AWX for centralized management and team collaboration * Custom module and plugin development * Security best practices and Ansible Vault

The True Value of Ansible

Beyond mere tools and syntax, Ansible empowers you with a new mindset:

- **Infrastructure as Code:** Your systems are defined with precision, versionable and shareable, propelling collaboration.
- **Focus Shifts:** Tedious manual work fades, letting you focus on strategic improvements and innovation.
- **DevOps Mindset:** Ansible bridges the gap between development and operations, fostering a culture of shared responsibility.

You are now an automation champion! Use your powers wisely, streamline your workloads, and unleash the full potential of both your infrastructure and yourself.

Thank You!

As an author, I'm thrilled to have guided you on this journey. Let's continue to make Ansible accessible to everyone!

Made in the USA
Middletown, DE
22 May 2025